FOUL DEEDS & SUSPICIOUS DEATHS AROUND SCUNTHORPE

TRUE CRIME FROM WHARNCLIFFE

Foul Deeds and Suspicious Deaths Series

OTHER TRUE CRIME BOOKS FROM WHARNCLIFFE

Please contact us via any of the methods below for more information
or a catalogue
WHARNCLIFFE BOOKS
47 Church Street, Barnsley, South Yorkshire, S70 2AS
Tel: 01226 734555 • 734222 • Fax: 01226 734438
email: enquiries@pen-and-sword.co.uk
website: www.wharncliffebooks.co.uk

Foul Deeds & Suspicious Deaths Around

SCUNTHORPE

STEPHEN WADE

Series Editor
Brian Elliott

Wharncliffe Books

First published in Great Britain in 2005
and reprinted in 2012 by
Wharncliffe Local History
an imprint of
Pen & Sword Books Ltd
47 Church Street
Barnsley
South Yorkshire
S70 2AS

ISBN 978 1 90342 588 6

The right of Stephen Wade to be identified as Author of this
work has been asserted by him in accordance with the Copyright,
Designs and Patents Act 1988.

A CIP catalogue record for this book is
available from the British Library

Typeset in 11/13pt Plantin by Mac Style, Beverley, East Yorkshire

Printed and bound in England
By MPG Books

Pen & Sword Books Ltd incorporates the imprints of
Pen & Sword Aviation, Pen & Sword Family History, Pen & Sword Maritime,
Pen & Sword Military, Pen & Sword Discovery, Pen & Sword Politics,
Pen & Sword Atlas, Pen & Sword Archaeology, Wharncliffe Local History,
Wharncliffe True Crime, Wharncliffe Transport, Pen & Sword Select,
Pen & Sword Military Classics, Leo Cooper, The Praetorian Press,
Claymore Press, Remember When, Seaforth Publishing and Frontline Publishing

For a complete list of Pen & Sword titles please contact
PEN & SWORD BOOKS LIMITED
47 Church Street, Barnsley, South Yorkshire, S70 2AS, England.
E-mail: enquiries@pen-and-sword.co.uk
Website: www.pen-and-sword.co.uk

Contents

Introduction

As historians have often pointed out, Scunthorpe is a very new town. It represents, for many, the quintessential urban story of the late-Victorian phase of the Industrial Revolution. In 1851 the total population of the five parishes which were eventually to become Scunthorpe was a mere 1,245 people. Those parishes of Crosby, Scunthorpe, Frodingham, Brumby and Ashby became Scunthorpe in the early twentieth century, and the population by 1936 was over 35,000.

Scunthorpe is a steel town, and since the rediscovery of lucrative beds of ironstone by Rowland Winn[1] in 1859 at Frodingham, its story has been inextricably connected to that industry. Only in recent years has it begun to diversify; the social history up to c. 1985 has been dominated by the string of works across the horizon. February 1981 was indeed a watershed, as the Normanby Park works closed down, and a few years later the unemployment figure for the town was around nineteen per cent.

Major investment and the massive building programmes that eventually united the parishes meant that what had been a cluster of villages at the beginning of the twentieth century became a 'gold rush' town a few decades later, as labour was rushed in from all areas of Britain. Many have called Scunthorpe a 'Frontier Town' and the tag it appears to carry in the comedians' repertoire is not deserved, as anyone visiting the place would immediately see that it is certainly not the dour, red-brick, seedy town one might expect from the comments of Jasper Carrott and others.

But this book is not only concerned with Scunthorpe. North Lincolnshire provides the wider setting, and the twenty mile radius around Scunthorpe takes in Gainsborough, Brigg, Barton and the Humber, the Isle of Axholme and reaches almost to the fringes of the Wolds. Although the sandy soils of Normanby and Frodingham may have been only a tiny and backward place in the mid-Victorian years, that is not to say that there have not been exciting and dramatic historical narratives around here. On the contrary, the very name, from *Scuma* (a personal name), is a clue to its Viking past, and the nearby Humber has been a haunt of pirates across the centuries. In 1536, the Pilgrimage of Grace began in earnest in Louth and Caistor. There were large movements of men across the Humber in these years, as the main leader of that revolt, Robert Aske, travelled to and fro between north Lincolnshire and east Yorkshire.

On the Western side of the town, only eight miles away, is the large village of Epworth, home of the Wesley family. Here, in the fiercely independent Isle of Axholme, there have been some unruly and violent episodes of northern history. One old legend speaks of the place as an independent kingdom in the Saxon period, and in the days when the fens were being drained by Vermuyden, there was serious trouble. The Dutch engineer settled near Sandtoft, where the locals burned down the chapel, driving out the foreigners, so they had to move to Hatfield. Even as early as the medieval period, there had been bother for the same reasons: a Selby monk, Gilfred, worked for decades to drain a part of Hatfield Chase. The local people saw this as the destruction of much of their source of flesh and fowl in the marsh, and they complained and took extreme action. After Gilfred's death all his work was ruined by locals.

It was a tough area and there were some savage crimes in these wild and untamed places: in Wroot in the Isle in 1767, a woman saw a servant girl being pursued by her mistress, who grabbed her, threw her down and beat her with her fists. But, as B J Davey points out in his book, *Rural Crime in the Eighteenth Century*, 'This was the darker side of eighteenth-century vitality. That spontaneous, lively, interpersonal violence of the public house and the street ...'

To the south, is the market town of Brigg, notable for the folk song *Brigg Fair*, referring to the famous horse fair which was first granted by a charter of King John in the early thirteenth century. Again, there were problems, as such events attract travellers and criminals. The *Stamford Mercury* in 1844 reported that:

the town seems to be the centre of mendacity: beggars and blacklegs were almost numberless... and were allowed to ply their trade without either fear or check from the Powers that Be.

But most of the crime revisited and retold here is focused on the steel town and its problems of law and order. What else could be expected when the area had to cope with massive numbers of workers coming into the town? What typifies this was the Anchor Project of 1969. This entailed the building of a central basic oxygen steelmaking plant and new mills for bloom and billets; and medium section steel. The end result was huge redundancies. But there were the boom times too. In the fifties there had been large-scale recruitment drives to such an extent that the works became known in some quarters as 'The Labour Exchange.'

The 'foul deeds' here then, range from rural crime such as arson to the familiar catalogue of urban offences, notably assault, armed robbery and murder. But within the general history of law and disorder there are always the specific crimes that relate to contemporary social problems, and these have a moral dimension, too. This is shown in the tragic stories behind the huge numbers of Lincolnshire people transported to Australia in the years up to 1867. Until Sir Robert Peel reduced the number of capital offences in the 1830s, there had been 220 capital offence crimes on the statutes, and the list of Lincolnshire convicts includes such items as:

Mary Burton, crime: house-breaking. Convicted in 1824 at Lincoln Assizes. Sentence: fourteen years transportation.
Richard Thornton, crime: obtaining goods by false pretences. Convicted at Kirton Quarter Sessions. Sentence: seven years transportation.

Of course, many of the crimes committed in the earlier part of the period covered here ended in execution, and these extreme cases, though few, again tell the historian a great deal about the nature of society at the time. One of the most tragic types of crime is infanticide, and a case at Covenham, near Louth, illustrates this. A Mrs Watmough killed a child that had been born to her, and her aim had been to escape shame and disgrace. The father was said to be 'a noted professor of religion', and Ann Watmough declared 'of sound mind.' The poor woman tried to end her own life while awaiting trial.

But other crimes also show how desperation and deprivation play their part. In the war years there was serious malnutrition in some areas, notably in Grimsby, and much crime was related to stealing food, often with violence. Towards the mid-twentieth century there was a massive rise in juvenile crime and in 1938 there was widespread discussion about whether or not Scunthorpe should have its own institution for housing young offenders.

Finally, there is the strand of crime that one can only call dramatic, with a dash of myth as well. Such are the stories of highwaymen and footpads (Dick Turpin himself crossed Lincolnshire, as he went north with his stolen horses). The myths are closely related to the crimes, as in the case of Poll Pilsworth of Epworth. In her day she was seen as a poisoner and a murderess. Today, there are theories as to some obvious reasons for the death resulting from the consumption of her baking. But her ghost is supposed to walk the path by Epworth churchyard, a restless soul in purgatory for her sins.

The confrontations and conflicts in this area are not new: from the reign of Henry IV through to that of James I, the Tyrwhitts and Rosses of Barton and Melton Ross continued a feud. In 1412 one of the worst instances took place when Sir Robert Tyrwhitt of Kettleby lay in wait for Lord Ross at Melton, with a force of five hundred men. Ross had been forcibly prevented from entering the manor. The case went to the high court and Tyrwhitt had to crave the king's pardon. A later skirmish resulted in many deaths and gallows were erected at Melton. Up to the 1850s the gallows were maintained.

I have lived in this area since 1974 and in that thirty years have been aware that the nature of crime has changed, but the same profoundly human stories go on at home and in the streets every day. These narratives from time gone by can still tell us a great deal about the way we live now.

High Melton today. The author

I would like to thank Brian Elliott, the series editor, for his help. Carol Longbone at Scunthorpe Central Library has been extremely helpful, and Detectives Mick Alcock and Charles Watkinson were a mine of information on the later cases. Laura Carter provided the line drawings and has helped to bring some of the people and places into the imagination. Barbara Hetherington provided valuable details on Peg Pillsworth's story. Special mention must be made of the pioneering work done by A A Clarke, in his two books on murder cases around the Humber (see Bibliography). Paul Kemp and Sue Edlington provided invaluable assistance and photographs for the *Newcastle Arms*, Gainsborough case.

Note
1. Rowland Winn, son of Charles Winn, Lord of the Manor of Frodingham.

CHAPTER 1

Smugglers, Pirates and Villains by the Humber

... there were pirate ships sailing this way from Dunkirk ...

I t is generally thought that today we have no 'capital punishment crimes' in Britain, but we do: the sentence is mandatory for the offence of piracy when murder is attempted. This is subject to the mercy of the royal prerogative. North Lincolnshire and its coast in the Humber estuary has seen plenty of this, and it is doubtful that much mercy has ever been shown to the villains involved.

In 2003, a piece in the Nostalgia supplement of the *Scunthorpe Evening Telegraph* gave an account of the Humber keel, the *John William*, and mentioned that in recent years it had been in the way when customs and excise had to unload a massive load of contraband cigarettes. Somehow, this modern anecdote fits into a long history of smuggling just north of Scunthorpe on the Humber shores.

Since about AD 500 there have been Viking boats raiding the shores, and there must have been hundreds of 'foul deeds' in those early Dark Age years not far from Scunthorpe and Burton. Over the centuries, the villages along from Burton to Barton have been involved in the traffic of political and insurgent factions, and there have even been pirates along that waterway.

In the early seventeenth century a pamphlet was published, giving an account of a particularly effective pirating fleet from the Middle East, and it is clear that this 'Sally fleet' as it is known, was part of a well-established network of villains around the Humber and the marshlands of Hatfield. In fact, at one time the expedition against these slave-gathering vessels was led by William Rainbarrowe, whose son had been brutally killed in Doncaster in 1648.

Edward Peacock, the local Victorian antiquary, relates that there were also pirate ships sailing this way from Dunkirk, and that these became known as 'Dunkirkes'. He also makes it clear that for centuries, the east Coast of Yorkshire and the Humber were open to attack in this way. Much of this history is as yet unresearched, but there is one story, from the Tudor period, that shows what these activities were like. Unbelievably, at that time, no less a person than the Abbot of Whitby was involved in dealing with these privateers and thieves from abroad. The Star Chamber investigation into his business uncovered the fact that he, John Hexham, was in league with a gang of disreputable characters, and that they all bought a ship in their enterprise. Piracy thus had a 'reputable' fence and name in the criminal transactions across the East Riding and North Lincolnshire.

The story of their robberies is a fitting one to begin this narrative of crime in the Scunthorpe area, as some of the articles this gang stole were then called 'osmands' and, as Edward Peacock tells us, these were 'the very best used for the finest purposes, such as arrow-heads, fish-hooks.... And the works of clocks.'

Smuggling in the area has a long history, too. When there was an embargo on the export of wool, for instance, in 1274, a group of Louth men sold sacks of wool to Flemish traders and (using bribes) got them to a port and away from home. There was a notably large-scale operation in this trade in 1785, when at Goxhill no less than ninety tons were put aboard ship to go to France. All that can be said about the piracy and smuggling of gangs through the centuries is that most of their stories are still untold, and the tales that were uncovered illustrate the extent of the trade: the fact that a man

Barton: the main road from Scunthorpe. The author

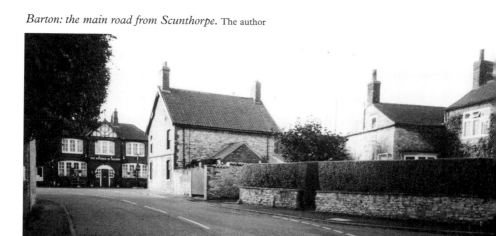

could be murdered in Doncaster because of a family link to one side of a faction tells us a great deal about the vendettas that could emerge from these nefarious dealings.

Nothing could really put a stop to this business; not even Sir Robert Walpole's Excise Bill of 1733, nor the formation of a corps of elite 'Riding Officers' in 1698, who could be joined by the dragoons if need be.

As the historian Roy Porter said, 'smuggling gave moonlighting employment along the coastal strips.' The fact is that the Humber provided one of the most hospitable and defensible areas for this kind of 'moonless' nightwork.

Another villain close to the Humber was undoubtedly Dean Fletcher and his very foul deed at Thornton Abbey, not far from Barton. In the late fourteenth century, the Abbot, Thomas de Gretham, was enjoying a liaison with his student, Heloise. In a complex plot involving the Abbot, a tough called 'The Green Devil' locally, and a stolen deed of land ownership, we have a tale of awful punishment, being inflicted on the Abbot by Fletcher (for 'lax living' according to one source) and the victim reputedly immured in the abbey.

In the 1830s, workmen found a secret room, where there was a skeleton on the floor, which turned to dust when touched. It was wearing a monk's habit. It most likely was the Abbot. But there are other candidates for the identity of the remains. A 1935 report talks of a certain Walter Munton who was also an 'evil liver.' As with most of Britain in the last decades of the fourteenth century, there was anarchy around. The 'Green Devil', whoever he was, was keen on robbery and pillage in the area: he had his own gang of followers and they were apparently feared by all in and around Barton.

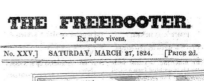

THE FREEBOOTER.

Ex rapto vivens.

No. XXV.]   SATURDAY, MARCH 27, 1824.   [PRICE 2d.

THORNTON ABBEY; OR, THORNTON COLLEGE, LINCOLNSHIRE.

Thornton Abbey. From a print of 1824

CHAPTER 2

Captain Cobbler and Robert Aske
1536

He [Robert Aske] *was dragged through York, but asked Bystanders not to pray for him.*

Few people around Scunthorpe and Burton-on-Stather today will be aware that in the 1530s, when Henry VIII and his repressive measures against common people and monastery land were raging, revolutionary leaders were travelling hastily across from Louth and Caistor to board a ferry or race towards important meetings in Doncaster. In 1536, a small army of men from Louth walked to Caistor and that village became a central focus in the story of the Pilgrimage of Grace.

In that year, as a Louth man called Nicholas Melton (a shoemaker) emerged as the leader of the local rebellion and became known widely as Captain Cobbler, there were murders done only fifteen miles from Scunthorpe.

The Pilgrimage accelerated as people had more than they could stand of a series of heartless and rapacious measures which were taken against the provinces: common land was being enclosed and so ordinary people lost rights to grazing and some of their food supplies; Henry had disposed of 1,593 areas of monastic land; direct and indirect taxes were summarily increased. Even worse, he was sending hard-nosed commissioners up north and north east, to extort possessions from the middle classes and bully people in general who were vulnerable.

Northerners (anyone north of the Trent/Severn line) felt very distant from government, and they were often written about as a blunt and barbarous people, part-savages. The grudges were mounting as people were executed for quite minor offences. Action needed to be taken, and it was in Lincolnshire that it all began. The catalyst was the punishment of a local man, the Vicar of Louth, Thomas Kendall. His profound beliefs were challenged and tested by the Henrician regime, and he gave a sermon that can only be described as an invitation to rebel. The church bells rang to communicate a rebellion, and they were rung backwards – a sign that there was trouble brewing.

Captain Cobbler started his work in earnest. He was the leader and he had the nucleus of a gang with him from the beginning. A rebellion across the Humber was heard of, and steps were taken to make a connection, for greater strength. A key figure came through now, one Guy Kyme. He became the link-man and messenger between Robert Aske's men in Yorkshire and Cobbler's Lincolnshire force. Soon, a huge mass of over 3,000 men was walking towards Caistor. This body was not to be crossed, and they had their first killing quite soon. A bunch of King's men were pursued and galloped away, but a servant of Lord Burgh's was grabbed and killed, beaten to death by the mob. Not long after, others were killed, including a man in Horncastle.

The activity in North Lincolnshire came to a head on Hambleton Hill near Market Rasen, and there were so many powerful men involved now, that the whole rebellion was escalating into a national event. It is at this point that Robert Aske made a connection with the Caistor and Barton area. On August 4 at Barton, Aske came off the ferry and, although we know only little about him, he was to have a massive impact on the Pilgrimage. He was a Yorkshireman, with land around Richmond, but also had connections with Aughton, near Howden. This made crossing to Lincolnshire an easy matter for him. In August he made links and associations; and by October he was moving south, passing through Sawcliffe, a few miles north of Scunthorpe, on his way to the Great North Road, accompanied by his nephews.

Aske made a union with the Axholme rebels, and found out that legally, the area around Burton was part of Yorkshire and thus he could appeal to a certain variety of local feeling, all helping the communication process. Aske was to spend a year in negotiations, playing political games, taking part in an accord at Doncaster, and even visiting the King himself at one point, with a guarantee of safe passage. But it was doomed to failure.

Aske was hanged in York in July 1537. We do not really know what happened to King Cobbler. He disappeared from the stage of history during this period. Aske died on market day, on Clifford's Tower. He was dragged through York, but asked bystanders to pray for him. Of course, skirmishes and reprisals went on for some time, but one of the most significant events in English history had had its beginnings and formed the hub of its communication network, just a few miles from Scunthorpe.

CHAPTER 3

Lawless Axholme

It could be summed up in the phrase 'stubborn independence'

T he area of Axholme, only eight miles to the west of Scunthorpe, has a history teeming with incident and myth, yet it has suffered from the fate of most borderlands in the chronicles: being neglected as neither one nor the other. Is it Yorkshire or Lincolnshire, or some of both? Records of the area often mention Cornelius Vermuyden, the seventeenth century Dutch engineer who managed to convert a large area of the Isle from marsh to good farming country, but even this advance, as Colin Ella makes clear, caused local rebellions and The Drainage saw 'sporadic rioting for almost a century.'

The land in question is along the Trent at the eastern side, from Amcotts down to Gunthorpe, and then to Crowle moors and Wroot in the west. In the centre of all this is the Wesley home of Epworth rectory, and even this place of pilgrimage has not been free of conflict and strife. Something about the Isle generates characters, but also a particular type of enmity and fierce local pride. Some account for the myths around the place by mentioning ley lines; but much of the explanation rests on the distance from any really large settlement in years gone by, and the insular nature of the attitudes bred. It could be summed up in the phrase 'stubborn independence.'

Even when Axholme had a brief self rule, in the Saxon period, there was murder. A deep rift between the Mercian king and Ornulff ended in the latter's banishment. He had had an affair with Elfrida, the proposed future king's wife. Ornulff, sent as an emissary, fell in love with her himself and they married and had a child. When he was told to come home, Ornulff wisely left the country and kept out of the way for a long time.

The story came to a head when Ornulff, in possession of a letter from the Pope, returned home, thinking that all would be forgotten. He was wrong: letter from the Pontiff or not, the man was knifed, and the tale is that Elfrida was ruined and crazed by this and soon the king was defeated. Ornulff's son reigned in Axholme following this. The story shows the basic northern tendency never to forgive and to bear a grudge forever, and that is probably the point of the tale, almost a parable.

The Wesley's home, a prominent tourist attraction today, on the south side of the village, is reputed to have its ghost, but aside from paranormal activity, the life of the Wesley family there tells us a great deal about the law and order – or lack of it – in the Isle in past centuries. Samuel, John's rector father, was always subject to his home and grounds being packed with parishioners rioting, barracking and making their objections to him known. The English custom of 'rough music' was rife then, and as Samuel Wesley was a hard man who treated his family (daughters in particular) unfeelingly, at times he was far from popular.

Part of this rural Lincolnshire rough music was the *stang nominy*: local women had their own ways of meting out justice to a partner who was violent to a spouse. In Epworth at that time it would have been the 'ran tan song' that explains this:

Now all ye old women, and old women kind,
Get together and be in a mind;
Collar him, and take him to the shit-house,
And shove him over head …

Added to this treatment would be the visit to the tannery where they would 'skelp' his backside. In Lincoln in 1556, a woman called Emma Kirkby was sentenced to a rough music punishment for adultery: she was to be 'ridden through the city and market in a cart and be rung out with basins.'

Nothing much changed in Victorian times: there was always the threat of riot and disturbance: in Axholme, at Owston, for instance, in 1873, a gang of youths caused fear and trembling in the church by rapping the pews, throwing wheat and yelling at everyone. In 1888, two men attacked a police constable; one of them fired a gun at the man and was lucky to do no harm. He was prosecuted for grievous bodily harm.

The Isle is on record as a place where violence settled many disputes and there is no doubt that rivalry between specific villages is at the heart of some of this. The Haxey Hood game on 6 January still commemorates the old traditions of rough and physical confrontation, as two villages gather all the men together and play a primitive version of football/rugby with a woman's hood.

Local historian, Colin Ella, sums up the Axholme history very well: he has summarised some of the crimes around Epworth, even back to the early seventeenth century, as recorded on the Court Rolls. The constables had a tough task, and perhaps the crimes recorded here are mostly concerned with maintaining the watch and the constables. It is surely symptomatic of the problems of the area when a certain John Fair was in court for failing to find a watch during a full day in June, 1625.

CHAPTER 4

Crime and cruelty in the Eighteenth Century

... he broke her leg in a brutal and vicious way, angling it over a doorway and stamping on it.

In the latter half of the eighteenth century it is not difficult to find forms of punishment that can never be squared with the civilised veneer of what has always been called the Age of Reason. In 1757 a woman was burned to death in York for adultery; at Tyburn another woman was burned for coining in 1789. Most of the many hangings that took place were for theft; by a 1736 law, servants stealing from masters could be hanged. In Scotland, in 1697, there had even been an execution for blasphemy.

It is hard to imagine the vulnerability of country people in the eighteenth century; there was no police force, merely village constables. Private law suits were the only course of action, and if a crime was committed against you, your next step was to find a constable and hopefully some witnesses as well.

In North Lincolnshire at this time, Scunthorpe was a tiny dot, along with other villages in the area. Luckily for most inhabitants of the area then, most criminals were inefficient and crime was mostly opportunist. There were highwaymen and footpads, of course. Dick Turpin himself was passing through Axholme to the Goole area around 1730. His favourite northern public house, the *Dragon* at Welton, is not too far north. But serious crime against the person was not common. For instance, in the 1770s, there were only six cases of murder at Lincoln Assizes, and only one resulted in an execution. In the same decade there were only eight robberies brought to court, and three cases of rape.

Historians have talked about the 'high level of personal violence' at this time, and the literature of the period certainly supports this. The novels of Daniel Defoe and Henry Fielding testify to the generally tough and aggressive society of rural

England up to the middle of the century. In the area between
Epworth and Barton, there were plenty of violent and nasty
assaults, in keeping with this trend. A typical crime of that era,
repulsive to the modern reader, is the story of one William
Paddison of Kirton Lindsey, who 'mayhemmed his wife' – that
is, he broke her leg in a brutal and vicious way, angling it over
a doorway and stamping on it. He was apparently set on
breaking her other leg but neighbours intervened. There was a
great deal of savage rage and assault in the family. One of the
most terrible has to be the Flixborough man, called Ellis, who
attacked his wife Sarah in a way that is beyond all reason. He
actually threatened her life on several occasions, but one day
set fire to the bed in which Sarah and their child were sleeping.
He lit a dry furze bush under them. People reported that
shortly before he had stalked her with a pitchfork, threatening
to kill her.

In Willoughton near Kirton, we have a typical case of a
crime against another vulnerable group – servants. A shepherd
and farmer there were brought to court by his servant, Mary
Baker. He had kicked and beaten her, punched her face and

Kirton in Lindsey today. The author

thrown her against a wall. It was so severe that she was in extreme pain for a week.

Murder, though not common, was often the result of attacks in the dark, in isolated spots, and North Lincolnshire did have its highwaymen. A little way north of Gainsborough a man was found dead in 1760; he had been brutally beaten and thrown to drown in a cold bath. He had been robbed of all possessions and there were bloody, gaping wounds on his head. What stresses the rarity of this is the furore it caused. The tale made the national newspapers, and there was a reward for the immense sum of £150 offered for information leading to a capture.

Repressive laws lead to occasional acts of desperation and rage against the officers of the law, of course. A justice at Caenby, Lawrence Monck, was a magistrate and also had property in London. He had come to the county through a profitable marriage (very much a good 'career' move then) and because he was involved in enforcing the Militia Act, there was general enmity against him. This act of 1757 had made justices find local men to be conscripted into the militia for a period of three years, and so was highly unpopular.

The mob came looking for him, to his own home, and planned to destroy his property and most probably harm him too. He seems to have been aware of the trouble brewing, as he at first fled to Lincoln. Later, though, he negotiated with them and plenty of drink and promises seemed to placate them. The *Moncks' Arms* public house, though derelict, still stands at Caenby Corner today as a memory of this.

But the reign of terror went on and a situation developed in which Monck and his family were repeatedly threatened and their own home attacked. He tried to buy them off with cash, and eventually constables were called out, but only with the duty of taking money to the trouble-makers. In the end, the justice took his frightened family to safety in Lincoln and remained there for a considerable time, having heard that other villages close by were now in rebellious mood.

Punishment was harsh in this misnamed Age of Reason period: between 1722 and 1799, ninety-one people were hanged in Lincoln, some for stealing sheep and some for

The Moncks Arms Hotel, *Caenby Corner: the one survival of the Monck name.*
The author

murder; one Mary Johnson was burnt to death for poisoning her husband. It comes as no surprise that offenders were often brutal; the society brutalised them.

CHAPTER 5

Poisonings in Epworth
1790s

*Her corpse was stretched across a plough sledge
and taken to the Burnham-Blow crossroads.*

Today, there would be plenty of reasonable scientific explanations given for the adulterated food that Poll Pilsworth possibly used in her baking in Epworth over two hundred years ago. But she may or may not have been the awesome poisoner she is reckoned to be, depending on your point of view.

A workhouse in the late eighteenth century, and in a quiet Lincolnshire village, must have been a desperately sad and repressive place. Any small comforts the inhabitants could have to ease their burden would have been welcome. In this story of a woman who may or may not have been a killer, we have someone who saw that tasty cooking was a small pleasure she could give to the unfortunates.

Poll was heavily built, a solid and industrious person working at the poorhouse in Queen Street. It has been recorded that in many ways she was of a kind and generous disposition, helping an old tinker of the area, and also being affectionate to children. The old travelling man would bring any gifts of food he had back to his wife at the poorhouse, but these would naturally be passed on to Poll, the cook.

Her favourite dish and speciality was a spice cake. For some time she must have been quite competent and reliable in her food preparation, but at this point, things went wrong. People started to die, and they were people who had eaten her spice cake: children and then the tinker's wife. Things escalated when the old man then fell ill, and his symptoms seem consistent with some kind of poisoning. Naturally, locals put two and two together and came up with a murderer in the village: Poll Pilsworth. When the old tinker died, action was taken.

Queen Street, Epworth, where the workhouse once stood. The author

As was the case in isolated areas of England then, gang law was the first law to be followed, and the mob went to find her. But Poll pre-empted this by taking her own life. She killed herself with poison, it seems.

But sometimes the stories of crimes have to be constructively criticised; her body was taken to a crossroads, following the old tradition for anyone with similar apparent evil to witchcraft. Her corpse was stretched across a plough sledge and taken to the Burnham-Blow Row crossroads. According to local historians, she was buried and stakes put through her heart. But was this a murder story?

Current thinking accounts for the fairly common occurrence of deaths through 'poisoning' as being down to adulterated wheat. Even today, farmers and health officials have stated that on many occasions, huge piles of adulterated wheat have to be burned, such is the danger to public health. This would seem likely, as there is one important factor missing in the story – the absence of a motive. Why would she kill poor people? Previous accounts had said that she liked the poorhouse children and was kind. But then she did commit

The cemetery, Epworth. Poll's bones are said to lie at this junction. The author

suicide, and the only explanation for this could be a certainty that she was finished; that no-one would believe her, and that similar examples of mob-rule had always led to dire and bloody punishments.

The worst scenario is that Poll took her life through guilt and remorse, but that seems unlikely. There could have been any one of a number of sources for bad food at that time. Perhaps the most likely explanation is the general climate of terror on the part of any poor and unprotected woman in such a position. The results of the deaths, regardless of the causes, would have been too much for the poor woman to live with. If this is so, then here we have a tragic story of a lonely and misunderstood person who was the victim of a cruel twist of fate, rather than a heartless killer who took perverse pleasure in poisoning innocents and helpless individuals. Murder sometimes borders on myth and superstition, and in this Epworth tale, there may be more than a modicum of folklore, not too dissimilar to witch stories from the countryside.

Poll took her own life, using digitalis.[1] We know her motive for that, but there seems to be no motive whatsoever for her to kill children. One final stunning detail is that Peg was buried with two stakes driven through her heart.

These were primitive times indeed, when science was cancelled out by irrational fears. Her bones lie at the junction of Blow Row and Burnham Road, thought of at the time as befitting nothing more than the lowest kind of murderer.

Note
1. A drug made from the dried leaves of foxgloves (digitalis).

CHAPTER 6

Arsenic and Mary Milner
1847

He [Dr Moxon] traced the remnants of the pancake from hearing that the dead woman had been vomiting in particular places.

Compared to the case of Poll Pilsworth, the account of Barnetby poisoner Mary Ann Milner presents no puzzle at all, and it also brings to light an exemplary piece of forensic investigation well before that line of work became a science. Barnetby is a beautiful and peaceful hamlet just beyond Brigg, these days en route to Humberside Airport. But in early Victorian times it was small and easily circumscribed: that is, everyone knew everyone else.

This aspect of life there made any kind of local misdeed something that was highly likely to be found out and fingers pointed in suspicion very soon after any suspicious action. Mary Milner, only twenty-seven-years-old, first killed her mother-in-law and attempted to kill her husband. The latter survived, but it was easy to see why she might do it. She stood to gain plenty of money, paid from a burial club. For this, she was cleared, as there was no actual evidence to prove conclusively that she put the poison in the food. The old woman died quite quickly, but the husband survived, paralysed on one side of his body.

The medical men did find arsenic in the stomach of Mary's mother-in-law, and there is a part jocular and rather sick story of the young woman buying the poison from Mr Percival in Barnetby. When he spoke in court, he recalled some pleasantries in talking to her, she referring to a rat problem and he commented that she did not look suicidal, so he should have no concerns in selling her the stuff. Perceval remembered that she had once had a dog who died through eating rat poison. Interestingly, the druggist also recommended that she take an antidote. He was clearly a careful man, who perhaps underneath the jocularity had some fears; his position was

The road into New Barnetby. The author

precarious in some ways if anything had come of this, because there was a high-level coverage of arsenic killings in the national and local press in this decade.

But the arsenic went in a meal of sage and gruel and the first victims went down. Sure enough, Mary withdrew some cash not long after the woman's death. But she would have been free and returned back to normal life, rather better off, had it not been for the suspicious death of someone else: a Mrs Hannah Jickels. In this case, there was no financial gain. The

Cobb Hall, Lincoln Castle, where criminals were hanged. The author

only explanation is that Mary did not like the woman. In this case the woman died from eating pancakes, and a long and elaborate questioning was given to ascertain the whereabouts of any remaining pancake mix, so studies could be done on them.

At this point, in steps Dr James Moxon of Brigg, clearly an enterprising and clever doctor. He traced the remnants of the pancake from hearing that the dead woman had been vomiting in particular places. Mary had tried to clean it all up and dispose of it on a nearby ash-heap, but Moxon followed the trail, did a simple test and found arsenic in the food. Twelve grains can kill an adult: Jickels had been given thirty. A local shoemaker, William Booth, had also joined in, and had found some pancake on a dung-hill.

There is no surprise that her dying was violent and shocking, a long and agonising torture before her eventual painful death. Jickels had actually told a friend that she had been poisoned by Mary Milner. Moxon had been suspicious of a possible poisoning case at first, when he had been present to attend the dying woman. Unbelievably, Mary had been in the room to watch the symptoms develop with Jickels, and had coolly said 'These are the same thing my mother died of ...'

Mary Milner was charged and convicted this time: she was sentenced to hang at the Cobb Hall drop, Lincoln Castle, but it was not to be. An unusually large crowd gathered (several thousands) and it was to be a public spectacle, but young Mary had hanged herself in her cell with a handkerchief. All through her trial, as the contemporary account said, she remained 'firm and collected ... nor did her demeanour alter when the jury returned their verdict.'

Mary Ann Milner never got to spend and enjoy the burial club money; her astoundingly stupid and clumsy attempts to follow up the first murder with a second that had no obvious motive led to her downfall.

CHAPTER 7

A Fatal Stabbing in Kirton
1847

... something happened that night to cause one friend to murder another.

J oe Travis and Charles Copeman were two young drinking friends who liked wandering around their favourites inns around Blyborough and Kirton. Just before Christmas, 1847, the famous Year of Revolutions in Europe, young Travis was about to do something that would cause something of a revolution in his own life: knife his friend Charles, a man about to be married. They had stopped in a field on the way home, and after a night of teasing and ribbing, something happened to cause one friend to murder the other.

The lanes and fields around this area are often dark and isolated; add to that the fact that both men had drunk a large amount of beer, and that opens up all kinds of possibilities for crime. After all, they were walking in the midst of rolling farmland, broad, open fields and hedgerows. The place was already riddled with superstition, and in years gone by many people must have been attacked in such lonely places around Kirton, on the escarpment up from the plain to the old Roman road to Lincoln.

It is known that Travis was in debt, and that Charles had some money on him: some silver coins. They left the *Greyhound* at Blyborough, and with Charles's little terrier in tow, they set off for the *Red Lion* in Kirton. The next morning, the body of Charles Copeman was found dead in the field, his throat cut, and there were many more knife wounds to his head and face. If it had been a case of a friends' fall out, then it entailed a considerably forceful and raging frenzy. Surely the gallows would almost have been ordered for Travis when his multi-bladed pocket knife was found nearby.

The dog was still by his master's body, and it took more than one man to move him away. It was a sign that this was not

The tiny village of Blyborough where Travis and his victim walked. The author

going to go away, even though young Travis had one thing on his side: there was no sign of any of his clothes, and they would have been very blood-stained indeed after that attack. The money had been stolen, after the man's pockets had been ripped open, and so fierce was the cut that it had severed the jugular.

But at Lincoln, Travis was acquitted. There had been no discovery of any clothes. Rumour has it that his mother had destroyed them, and one report even claims that she wore her guilty son's clothes under her own during the course of the investigation, just to be sure that there was no possibility of discovery. Astonishingly, he walked free.

Now there comes a stunning twist to the tale: not long after this Travis was drinking at the *George* when he had a shock: there had been a witness that night. As they sat in the public house, the newspaper out to be read around the table recounting the tale of Travis's release, a bricklayer called Bill Fell spoke out that in fact he could have claimed the huge reward of £100. He had been in the very same field where the killing took place and had seen everything. Fell had rowed with his wife and taken off into the night. Ultimately, he lay by a haystack in the murder field. The puzzle is why he had not come forward before, and the only explanation would be that he had something to hide, perhaps a liaison of some kind.

This turn of events made Travis tell a different tale, and it was elaborate. He could not be tried again for the offence, but he was tried for robbery. Now Travis told the most unlikely story that they had been 'acting the goat' and that it all got out of hand, ending with Travis swinging a punch at his friend, forgetting that he had his knife in his hand and was about to clip a cigar. Obviously, a one-stroke swing at a face could hardly result in multiple facial wounds and a deep gash across a major artery. The only excuse for this given was that if he wounded him more, it would look as though he had been attacked by a footpad. The place where all this happened is very hard to find now; the Greyhound is no longer at Blyborough, which is now only a farm and a few houses.

The town was not a good choice for such an offence: Kirton at that time had a House of Correction and the town was remarkably well organised in that respect, taking the whole business of penology very seriously, even to the extent of installing a tread-wheel and providing a surgeon and a string of carefully chosen governors.

Lady Luck smiled on Travis again; he was sentenced to transportation. But this was not to last for long. He died on board ship, just a few days into the voyage towards Australia.

CHAPTER 8

Six Months for Manslaughter at Barton
1851

*Thompson was beaten mercilessly,
in a frenzied attack.*

This case is so unusual that it would most likely not have been allowed to be called a 'crime of passion' even in France, and it contains such a stroke of luck for the offender that it offers a rare glimpse into the workings of the law in the nineteenth century.

Fleetgate in Barton is a long, narrow road leading from the centre of town down to the waterside. Now it still has plenty of older buildings along its edge and a few small homes. In the mid-Victorian period, one of the dwellers in Fleetgate was a carpenter called Sanderson. As with so many killers, there was a certain variety of local reputation that drew on a side to his character that has no bearing at all on this murderous tale: he was known as Happy Jack.

There was nothing happy about him when it came to his wife. There is nothing on record to suggest that he had any good reason to be jealous of her, but he was insanely so, and his behaviour led to some obsessive and erratic actions. People at the time must have seen that his too-vigilant and aggressive attitudes to her would lead to something serious, and it did.

This was on a dark evening in 1851. Sanderson was startled by the sound of gravel being thrown against the window. Little could be so stereotypical of a lovers' tryst, and he sprang into action, assuming that his wife and lover were trying to communicate. He dashed outside to look around and he saw a man called Thompson, who worked on the New Holland line as an engine driver. No questions were asked, just immediate and very extreme action against the man, yet it may not even have been Thompson who threw the gravel.

Sanderson had a poker in his hand and he caught the man close to Credland's wall. Thompson was beaten mercilessly, in a frenzied attack. It took him several days to die, and this was from a fractured skull. He was carried home after being found lying in his own blood on the pathway. If anyone saw all this, they said nothing or did nothing at the time.

Now the amazing twist of fate occurred. The case was being undertaken by the Magistrates' Clerk, Mr Graburn, and the Reverend Charles Barton, the Rector of Saxby. Incredibly, they paid a call to the bedside of the dying man, and from that point there emerged a disgraceful scene. They began to argue and this became most heated. It must be recalled that they had

Fleetgate, Barton. The author

gone to the home in order to note down a statement that would be vital evidence for the court. Instead of proper official business, a war of vanity began. The Rector was having legal procedure explained to him by the clerk, and his pride was affronted.

When Barton spoke the words, 'When I want the advice of a mere clerk I will ask for it ...' everything intensified into a slanging match. Barton raved and screamed at the clerk, and all this in the same small room as a man who was suffering a slow and painful death. It did not end there; the clerk filed an official complaint against the Rector. It was not only unprofessional conduct, but could have been construed as obstructing the process of law. The statement argued that the churchman should have no right to continue his duties on the bench.

The result of all this is something that arguably explains the bizarre sentence passed on Sanderson: manslaughter and therefore six months imprisonment. Six months in Lincoln Castle would not be pleasant, but the fact is that this was a jealous husband who went in pursuit of his victim with an

Barton: the main through road. The author

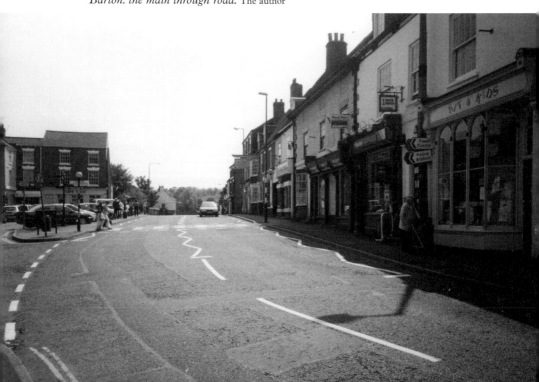

intent, if not to kill, then to cause severe bodily harm. But the clerk's letter and grievance were discounted, and the only explanation seems to be, as local writer Karen Maitland comments, that the Rector had gained some insight into the state of mind experienced by the man in the dock – and was 'inclined to have every sympathy with Sanderson ...'

The wife was lucky in her choice of friends; or, she lived in a community with a firm sense of self-help and support. Otherwise, she would almost certainly have been killed. We do not know for sure what the man's war experience had been, but the modern mind would probably try to find reasons for this homicidal fit. The Victorian Age was not so sensitive.

CHAPTER 9

Ralph, the Prison Houdini
1854

... to some law officers, there was nothing romantic about this violent man.

Before the prison system was more extensively developed, late in the nineteenth century, there was a widespread method of using lock-ups in villages and towns, together with Houses of Correction. It has to be recalled that the rural police force in the middle years of the Victorian period was still only partially structured and streamlined. For all these reasons, there was a reliance on a House of Correction in most areas (such as one in Kirton Lindsey) and on small lock-ups, often the room by the local constable's own house, as was the case in a village like Hibaldstow.

With this in mind, it is not surprising that there were escapes, and the tales of these desperate adventures and journeys often read like fiction. This is the case with a hardened and sly criminal called Joseph Ralph. In 1854 he was given a sentence of twenty years' transportation for a burglary offence. From that point his life reads like a tale from a Dick Turpin romantic adventure.

Ralph was an imposing figure. When the local paper printed the escape notice concerning the escape of the thief from Lincoln, it was pointed out that he was under sentence for transportation for twenty-five years, and that he was around thirty years old, quite short, and had 'a full round face, flesh colour, small mouth, and rather small blue eyes. He had a small mole under one eye, and light brown hair 'with a tendency to curl'. When last seen he was dressed in dark grey trousers and a prison waistcoat, and he even had silk boot-laces. A reward was offered.

Nevertheless, to some law officers, there was nothing romantic about this violent man. The first vanishing act on record is his escape from Lincoln Castle – a remarkable feat.

He used the familiar trick of arranging his bed so that a 'sleeper' appeared to be lying in it when inspected, and then found a way out under the eyes of the officers. The man has to be commended for inventiveness and daring here. But he immediately resumed his nasty ways and robbed a house to steal silver. In Barton he was tracked down and taken captive, but only after a desperate struggle involving a knife-fight. He was collared at the ferry, about to go across to Hessle, by constables Jubb and Clayton. Even with some help from a man called Sam Godfrey, he still put up a fight. In the struggle, Ralph opened a clasp knife and gave Godfrey a severe gash on the thigh, and he caught constable Jubb on the wrist. Clearly, he was there to take a ferry and move well away from the North Lincolnshire in which he was well known to the establishment.

The *Lincolnshire Times* reported that Ralph was very talkative and loved to brag about his thieving. He talked about several burglaries done around the Barton area. In fact, on the day of his capture, a great deal of his booty from these exploits was found on his person. The fact is, he may well have escaped the

The police station, where Ralph would have spent a night. The author

capture in Barton if it had not been for Clayton, who was a powerfully-built man and resolute in the extreme. He wanted his man and he kept hold of him.

In Lincoln Castle again later in the year he was clapped in irons, so it would seem that he was now firmly in place and unable to do very much or influence anyone to help. But amazingly, he somehow exchanged clothes with an unfortunate lunatic prisoner called Baines, and he even contrived to have a replica key made. Then, able to unlock the irons with which he was strapped to the prison wall, but still with irons on his arms, he made a blanket ladder and hopped out and over the wall. This appears to be all the more remarkable as a new separate system of imprisonment conditions had been introduced in 1840, in which inmates were put in a sound-proof cell and were only allowed to speak to the chaplain. Maybe he found a way around that procedure, as he did so many others.

Later, it was revealed that on the night of his escape from Lincoln, he robbed a place in Torksey, and that a butcher's smock he had stolen was found in a field near Fenton. Even more sensational at the time was the discovery that he had been responsible for a crime done before this, and attributed to one Jacob Freeman; the poor man waited quite a while to be exonerated.

Like the Scarlet Pimpernel, he pops up almost anywhere on the run, and at Trent Bridge he was too forward or at least too suspicious in his demeanour, and when a policeman started asking awkward questions he let his fists to the talking and there he was, under arrest yet again.

Ralph still wasn't finished and managed to grab some tongs to use as a weapon against the officers. It is entirely understandable that this desperado was sent to Armley Gaol in Leeds. He was back in his native Yorkshire, having been born in York somewhere around 1824. He had grown to be too much of a handful for the rural forces and he was given to the professionals in handling hard cases. Tried at Lincoln in 1855, he was given an eighteen month sentence to be served in Lincoln Castle again, and then packed off to Australia. He would have then had the prospect of around one hundred and twenty days at sea, a regime of starvation food and little time on deck, if at all. Even Ralph would have found escape a tall order there.

Ralph's life and adventures read as dramatically as any story in a *Penny Dreadful*. But the romance is taken away when one recalls his savagery.

CHAPTER 10

Convict Stories
c.1800–1860

... in some cases there is a story available that accounts for these crimes and the system in more detail.

Between 1788 and 1840 over 110,000 men and women were transported to Australia. From among this body of people, almost 1,500 were from Lincolnshire. In the next twenty or so years until transportation stopped, another 50,000 were sent. Very few of these were political prisoners, and most were from the labouring classes. A prisoner was in for a very hard time, going first from Lincoln Castle to the hulks, the prison ships in the estuary. A third of the prison population in a hulk died in that place. In the year 1865 alone, 561 convicts arrived in Australia.

Port Arthur Penitentiary, Tasmania, where many convicts ended up. The author

Records of sentences issued at Lincoln show such cases as Samuel Keeble, twenty-seven, who stole four sovereigns and was transported for life, or two labourers who stole a brown mare and were transported for life. In North Lincolnshire, close to Scunthorpe, a seaman was given seven years transportation for stealing a silver watch. Some were luckier, such as the young girl who was sent to Gainsborough House of Correction for a small theft; but poor Mary Smith, guilty of petty larceny, was sent to 'some place beyond the seas for the term of seven years.'

Not much is known of many of these poor individuals, but in some cases there is a story available that accounts for these crimes and the system in more detail. An example is Thomas Gray, a man who stole a horse at Gainsborough in 1837. His effrontery when in the dock was remarkable, as he actually explained that he had a saddle and bridle in the hands of a Sleaford pawnbroker, and could he have the money please? He was angry at Justice Littledale's refusal to allow this, and for a strong remonstrance from the bench. If anything, the 'foul deeds' in this context were done by the government's legal system, as the Gainsborough Assize that same year were mostly petty offences: Samuel Sharpe stole two rams and was transported, and James Toynton for sheep-stealing.

Yet transportation of some of the villains in this area was in fact a desirable alternative to the noose. There were murders for which the killers were transported for life, such as Edward Bowring, who attacked a man with a knife and cut his stomach open, or young Samuel Kirby, only fourteen-years-old, who murdered his master. The young apprentice had been severely reprimanded for some fault and then sent to bed. But the young man had apparently poisoned his master. At first he was surely to be hanged, but public feeling was so clamouring and insistent that this was commuted to life transportation.

As the Victorian years advanced, the various penal reforms meant that there were gradually fewer offences with a mandatory death penalty, and the option of transportation was used in more of the severe cases. One important variety of offence was prominent in 1830s, though, and explains some of the severity of the sentences. These were the Captain Swing

Riots, a rural movement against mechanisation. Steam-driven machinery was driving out manual labour to a certain extent and Lincolnshire was one of the places affected. These led mostly to crimes against property such as destroying machines and rick-burnings, and the Whig government brought two thousand people active in the Captain Swing Riots to court. This was a case of mass fodder for the hulks and ships.

What the convicts would have looked like. The author

Lincoln was not untouched by these national movements, and a widespread riot in Lincoln raged at that time; for most of the villages and towns in North Lincolnshire, the riots were more often related to drink rather than political reform: in Gainsborough in 1839, for instance, probably as the Captain Swing phase was in the air, there was the case of the Beckingham Road rioters. This crowd took a boat across the Trent and were out to cause trouble. They were not disappointed.

But overall, many of the extreme crimes committed around Scunthorpe, Kirton and Brigg at this time resulted in many people being sent to either die miserably on board ship or to suffer in the terrible penal settlements of Van Dieman's Land. Surely what best sums up the pathos in all this is the case of Joseph Smith, aged twenty-two of Haxey, who stole a pony and was transported for life. The charges brought in this age are sometimes incredible: one Christopher Maxey, aged twenty, was acquitted of the charge of setting fire to a stack of mustard seed straw. He was very lucky not to be on board ship heading for Van Dieman's Land.

Yet modern historical research in the Van Dieman's Land connection, has highlighted some of the lives of Lincolnshire convicts in the Antipodes. For instance, William Wright was a soldier and gamekeeper near Lincoln who was convicted in 1828 for stealing a gun. We now know that he went on to become Overseer for Waterworks and Constable in Hobart town, Tasmania, and that this progession and 'second life' was not that unusual.

CHAPTER 11

Arson in the Villages
1861

There was a powerful regimental campaign against arson, such was the fear and terror it evoked.

Today, arson carries a maximum sentence of life imprisonment. It is criminal damage 'without a lawful excuse.' In rural areas, it has always been a profoundly serious crime. In the eighteenth century in North Lincolnshire, it was very rare; there were only two cases recorded in the latter decades. Historical periods patently have their own specific varieties of crimes against the property, some politically motivated and some factional.

Anyone wanting to set fire to a haystack in this area would not find the task difficult in the nineteenth century; rural fire-fighting was basic in the extreme and would be distant from any one the settlements of any size around Scunthorpe, Frodingham and Crosby at this time. This helps to explain the special fear and panic associated with a cry of 'fire'.

Around Scunthorpe one of the worst times for terrible incendiary crime was in the years 1860–65. There had been burnings during the Captain Swing years thirty years before this; but isolated arson still occurred and was deeply disturbing, as in the case of a farmer in Waddingham in 1855, when a rick was burned and everyone went out in search of suspicious-looking tramps. But in 1861 in the early hours of the morning on 8 September, it was the village of Belton, just five miles away from Scunthorpe, which was hit. It happened in Robert Robinson's stackyard and little could be done to stop the blaze. Although many of the residents came out to help they were not able to prevent three stacks being lost.

In the confusion of all this, it was noticed that a drunken man, Thomas Cawkwell, was there, trying to help in the fire-fighting. But later, in the cold light of day, when questions

The road into Belton, where the fires were serious back in 1861. The author

were asked and the constable looked around the site, footprints were found going from a rick to a field of root vegetables. These prints matched the boots worn by Cawkwell. There was a story behind the affair, involving a personal vendetta. The young man had been making advances to one of Robinson's servants and the farmer had made it clear that he wanted nothing to do with Cawkwell, and that he should stay away. Villagers had heard Cawkwell loudly vowing to get even and make the farmer pay for this rebuff. Apparently, this was not as effective as it might at first seem, as a blacksmith who said he heard this was not a trustworthy witness, being an ex-prisoner.

The Cawkwell family obviously had a drink problem; the man's father was drunk and slurred his words in court, and also when questioned by police officers. Justice was done in the end, though: Cawkwell was sentenced to twelve years penal servitude. It must have been a shock for Robinson to see the young man there, helping, in the crisis. He would have been more likely to impede progress, as so often happened in arson cases where the victim was generally unpopular.

There was a powerful regional campaign against arson, such was the fear and terror it evoked. An official, poster of 1865 refers to a series of arson cases across North Lincolnshire, including on properties at Thornton Curtis, Barton, Appleby and Worlaby. The poster offers a pardon to anyone turning evidence. Finding a 'grass' was always the quickest way to help basic police work to progress. In most cases, these extreme actions were taken because of a rankling grudge or sense of offence. Many of the explanations for this uneasiness can be found in the tough labour relations of the time, notably the pay and conditions experienced by agricultural labourers. This was the day of the hiring-fair and the master's total power in the contract. It was not until 1872 that Joseph Arch created the first agricultural workers' union.

In the end, the general trend of crime against property decreasing when food prices were cheap applies, but arson was always the exception to this, and this is one reason why it was one of the capital offences in the famous Bloody Code – the capital statutes rooted in the late seventeenth-century legislation. We have to remember that arson had been a serious problem in many counties in the Victorian period, and most prominently in the Eastern counties from Suffolk to the Humber shore.

CHAPTER 12

Attempted Murder by Civil War Veteran
Barton 1869

The affair came to a head when he set about her in a rage.

ohn Sinclair, a shoemaker of Barton, had certainly seen some of the world; he had fought on the Confederate side in the American Civil War (1861-1865). But if he is remembered at all it is for something despicable rather than any heroism he may have shown in battle on foreign shores. This is because Sinclair, forty-six at the time, tried very hard to knife his wife to death. He only failed to do so because the woman had friends to watch over her. If he had been a wandering adventurer, it did nothing to create anything noble in his character.

Sinclair had obviously been an absentee husband for some years, and his reasons for seeing combat are unclear. But the fact remains that when he came home, he was determined first to maim, and later to kill his wife. On several occasions he was thrown in gaol to keep him from the attempt. The affair came to a head when he set about her in a rage. The pair lived in Fleetgate and thankfully, Sinclair's wife, Jane, had friends and neighbours around. One of these, a relative of Jane, protected her on the night in question. The night before the major confrontation, he had thrown Sinclair into the street, and the man came back again, armed with a knife.

Todd restrained him and threw him down again, but Sinclair was quickly up, knife in hand, and went for Jane with some alacrity. Todd held him again, this time pinning him down and holding his throat until help came. When William Coulam came in they could handle the madman, but there was blood on Jane and she was in distress.

When the doctor, John Morley arrived, he inspected Jane and as she lay on a sofa, he noted a deep wound on her left

High Street, Barton The author

side; so severe that he stated that 'fat was protruding from the lips of the wound.' He cut her stays and started emergency treatment. The men had dragged Sinclair outside by this time. The worst was thankfully over.

In Barton magistrate's court the next week, Sinclair was ill and had to be given a chair. A sorry tale of his outrageous behaviour then emerged. Jane Sinclair was well enough to be a witness, and she related his actions. Sinclair, on his first appearance to challenge and threaten her, had said he would see her in prison as she had been 'in the family way' when he left for abroad. His attack on Jane that night had been extremely vicious. She said that after the assault she had felt as if her 'back was like to break.'

The neighbour, Coulam, a bricklayer, said that he heard the commotion and came in, finding the poor woman 'crudled by the back door.' Coulam helped her to a chair and saw that she was in awful pain. He had been called when another woman

Barton: where cries for help were heard. The author

had run into High Street and shouted, 'Will none of you come in? We shall have murder here tonight if not ...'

Another witness heard Sinclair on another occasion say something that suggests the man had lost hit wits. He had said that Jane Sinclair had poisoned a child of his. He said, 'They have poisoned a child of mine and Mrs Bethell, and before I've done I'll wash my hands in their blood.'

The man was in for another long prison stretch and was in fact insane. Pathetically, he said so himself in his last words in court: 'I am not drunk, but mad.' He had attacked his wife with a downward thrust of the knife and very narrowly missed piercing her heart. Whatever skills with weapons the man had learned abroad, and even in battle, served him not one iota back home in England. If anything, he was surely one of the casualties we would now label with a 'post-war stress syndrome.'

CHAPTER 13

The Landlord Kills his Wife
Owston Ferry 1883

James grabbed a knife and set on her, with Mary running out into the kitchen to scream 'Murder!'

J ames Anderson was a man with a violent temper and a rabid hatred of his wife. His brutal slaying of her at their home in East Ferry led him to the gallows. The story begins with James as a pub landlord in Owston Ferry, and life with his wife, Mary, seems to have always been difficult. It is clear that he was always nasty to her, and that he was a short-tempered, tetchy man. He was physically aggressive and at a time when wives were particularly vulnerable. In late Victorian England, no-one knew too much about 'stress' or even the psychology behind acts of physical brutality.

But when they moved across the Trent to live in East Ferry, things went from bad to worse. So intimidating was James that his wife would take the ferry back over to find some protection in the company of her son when things were intolerable. The son was kind and supportive, doing the right thing for those days – giving his malicious father a pasting. He took him on and meted out some family law. But instead of putting things right, the matter ended up in court, with James actually prosecuting his son for assault.

On 6 December came the fatal day. Events came to a head in the Anderson home. Their nephew, John Wood, had moved over the water to live with the son, and when he came over to pick up some clothes, he found that there was a major row in progress. Mary was shouting accusations of infidelity and James was obviously being inflamed to a rage well beyond his control. James grabbed a knife and set on her, with Mary running out into the kitchen to scream 'Murder!'

Imagine the scene when young John found them grappling on the kitchen floor. He immediately ran out and called for

East Ferry today. The author

some assistance. In just a few minutes, coming back, he saw his aunty staggering out, bleeding at the neck. It was a snowy day and she fell down, a trail of blood behind her on the pure white-coated street. She had even tried to reach a boat and get across to safety on the other side.

Now, James was so bursting with anger that his demonic urges made the Mr Hyde in him turn the blade on himself and drag it across his throat, before the eyes of young John, who had walked back inside. He was ranting that all this hell was down to Mary, for provoking him.

But he was destined not to die on that bloody floor. James recovered and was shut up in gaol. He was reported to have said, 'If the knife had been sharp enough for the task, I would have cut my head off.' But there he was, still alive, and sealed up in Lincoln gaol, then a new place only ten-years-old. When his brother went to visit him, he simply said that he was guilty of the awful deed and that he would pay the ultimate price. 'If the judge was to ask for a reprieve for me,' he said laconically, 'I would ask him not to, for I want to die for it.'

The view across the Trent from East Ferry. The author

The only issue left to resolve was whether or not James planned the killing, and therefore whether it was actually a case of murder. A reduction to manslaughter never happened and the ultimate penalty was imposed. On went the judge's black cap.

There was an appeal to the Home Secretary, and amazingly there were people in Owston Ferry and East Ferry who were in support of this appeal. We have to wonder what sort of reputation James and his wife had had for many years before this tragic conclusion to their married life came about.

The Horncastle executioner and shopkeeper, William Marwood, had recently perfected his humane 'long drop' hanging method and now he had a condemned man on whom

Lincoln Prison, built in 1872. The author

to try this out. In the death suite on 19 February, James Anderson must have prayed for forgiveness, but nothing could save him from the rope and on that day Marwood proved his skill. Anderson was the first man to die in the new prison on Greetwell Road. The hangman had already become notorious after hanging one of the Phoenix Park murders of 1882. The killer was to be sent from this world by a hangman who used a business card and headed his letters, 'Mr William Marwood, executioner, Church Lane, Horncastle.' In his career he was to hang almost four hundred criminals. He was cool and professional, to the extent of hanging a man one day and writing home to his wife the next, asking after his dog, Nero.

William Marwood, the Horncastle executioner. Laura Carter

WILLIAM MARWOOD.

CHAPTER 14

Indecent Assault – or Lies?
1890

It was the beginning of the end for the tradesman's reputation, guilty or not.

Israel Barratt was a Gainsborough outfitter, doing his business in Church Street. He was prosperous, and a believer in the very strong Victorian work ethic. He could even afford to pay domestic servants, and in the case of one of these, a young girl called Ellen Taylor, something happened to turn his life around and virtually ruin him. Whether he committed a crime is still open to doubt.

Ellen was only fifteen when she came into his home to work as a domestic servant. She had had posts in service before, but did not seem to stay long at particular places. On the day that trouble began brewing for Israel, in early September 1890, Ellen was making the beds upstairs, rather strangely, as the children slept. As she walked out onto the second-floor landing, she alleged that she met Israel and that he first asked her to go and fetch some meat for him, but then he grabbed her, according to her statement made later, and did 'improper things to her person.' Was it a case of indecent assault? It certainly looked that way for some time.

Ellen claimed that she shouted loudly as he molested her, and that she yelled that she would tell his wife. No-one responded to her cries. The man then seems to have cooled down, and retreated to the very top garret, while the girl went down to the ground floor – and here she, rather amazingly for future medical and legal debate, continued with her work.

The girl said that her employer then came down, obviously after doing some soul-searching about the supposed assault, and apologised to her, insisting that if she said nothing, the action would never be repeated. But if anything had happened, he had chosen the wrong victim. Ellen went to take the children for a walk and paid a visit to her mother, to whom she told the tale. It was the beginning of the end for the tradesman's reputation, guilty or not. Both her parents went to visit Barratt that very night, and it appears that there were negotiations and certain monetary suggestions that would avoid any further fuss.

But the case went to court. Mr Barratt was insistent that he had done nothing, and did not offer cash. When Ellen was cross–examined she told a garbled tale. The account now referred to being 'thrown onto the stairs' and that she was fighting for her breath in the struggle. She also said now that she did not scream. What happened next is very familiar in modern cases of a similar nature. The lawyers tried to 'dish the dirt' – searching for any implication of a laxness of character on her part. It was noted that the girl had had 'improper relations' with a young man a few months before her work with Barratt.

She had been employed by a Mr Walton, a pawnbroker, and there had been no complaints made there. The defence were looking for a clear narrative of the girl and her family looking for easy profits from alleged assaults, hoping nothing would ever reach a court. When employed by Walton, she had never said that she was over sixteen, so the notion that she might be playing another sort of game was dismissed.

This is an important point, as, at this time, the issue of child seduction and sexuality was very much a hot topic. Only fifteen years before this, the journalist W T Stead had set out to 'buy' a child to highlight child prostitution. His phrase, 'maiden tribute' would have been lodged in the middle class respectable mind with regard to Ellen's father's behaviour.

Barratt had made things much worse for himself by going to visit the girl and her family on the next evening after their visit to him. He said that he had meant no harm, and that he had been misunderstood. The girl's father's response had been put plainly: 'Now can you square this?' The father had also produced the daughter's birth certificate as well, showing that she had been born on 9 August, 1875. So she was indeed under sixteen and was a minor. He went on to say all the things that the defence would have pressed: that the girl had never been in a reformatory school, and that indeed was a 'good and proper behaving daughter.'

Barratt could only repeat that he had not taken any liberties with the girl, and the medical expert called; Dr Henry Wright, could really say no more than that the girl's condition at the time was no more than that she was 'red-eyed' and 'very badly shaken'.

The first hearing had ended dramatically, with Barratt saying to the police, 'I expected some bother – I wired for my father this morning.' Then he was locked up. The whole farrago led to a trial in which nothing was resolved, but he avoided a prison sentence. What did fade away for good was his good name. Reading the story today, everything balances uneasily on the cusp between being a sly attempt at extortion and the possibility that the man perhaps fondled the girl and realised very quickly the error he had made. It seems doubtful that he attacked her or was rough with her at all. The father comes across as a somewhat Dickensian character, full of dodges and ruses; he may well have been using the child as a means of squeezing cash from the middle class men of the area. But we will never know the truth.

CHAPTER 15

Poisoning at the *Newcastle Arms*
1892

The poor man had suffered a tetanic fit and as he was put on the couch, he was in convulsions.

om Morley was a familiar sight around the Gainsborough area. He had been an apprentice in the Hull grocery business, but since coming to Lincolnshire he had been making his money as a professional gambler. The mystery of his death may well be related to that often risky occupation, and he may well have made an enemy of Alexander Morgan, his murderer.

The killing was done by poisoning, and what is most puzzling about this complicated case, it was done in public: in the bar of the *Newcastle Arms* in Casketgate Street. The amazingly complex and indefinable personality of Alex Morgan gave the reports of this remarkable story many bizarre twists and turns as it came to trial.

The Newcastle Arms, *Gainsborough (centre).* Paul Kemp collection

The *Newcastle Arms* had been opened in 1838, and was named after the Royalist general of the Civil War. It was let in 1859. Records show there was a room called the sot's hole: it was a resort of hard drinkers, with twelve rooms in all.

The night of Morley's death began with an apparently amicable arrival at the public house with Morgan and with a woman called Booth. All witnesses say they engaged in friendly banter and there was no suggestion in their demeanour that an argument or confrontation might follow. Even more paradoxical, after Mrs Booth had left, all were sober and the poisoning happened suddenly. Morley became increasingly ill, and the people around tried to walk off his stomach cramps. Morgan said he would go and fetch a doctor, but he never came back, and the victim shouted out that he had been poisoned by his associate. Two local men, Robert Broadberry and a friend, did all they could; when two doctors arrived they gave an antidote but it was too late.

Morley died, with marked rigidity and other symptoms that made Mr Methven sure the poison given was strychnine. The poor man had suffered a tetanic fit and as he was put on a couch, he was in convulsions. In this state, he had managed to say, 'It's the white powder Morgan gave me!'

Morgan was charged a few days later, and it was a case of wilful murder. William Brown, the landlord of the *Newcastle Arms*, confirmed that Morgan had said he was going for help but never returned. But the doctor found white powder on the bar, and this was strychnine. He confirmed that the first clue to the nature of the poison was the free-flowing blood, having no coagulating tendency.

From the point that Morgan was imprisoned in Lincoln awaiting trial, to the first hearing, there were sensational developments. First, the whole tale of how the strychnine was acquired was told: an amount much larger than normal had been bought with the ostensible reason of killing two dogs. This had been done, and a very cautious druggist named Collett did the right thing and stopped a passer-by who knew Morgan to sign the official statement before administering the ten grains. The reason for the large amount was that 'There is often some waste in giving it.'

But contradicting this was a statement that a man had been sent to Collett with four shillings to buy poison (again for killing dogs). So was Morgan present or not? The more we read of Morgan, the less his behaviour makes sense, and one contemporary reporter made a dramatic story from the view that the killer had *delirium tremens*. If he had not been in full control of his actions, then it was hard to dismiss the evidence of an old man who had heard the two men's talk that last night of Morley's life as they walked from the *Peacock Hotel* to the *Newcastle Arms*. The old man had heard Morley say, 'I've letton on you and I mean to have it out of you before we

Church Street, Gainsborough. The author

Caskett Street, Gainsborough, where the Newcastle Arms *once stood.* The author

leave ...' This tantalising fragment of talk suggests a debt, and the man was a character who lived by gambling and lending cash. Was the motive therefore the simplest way to avoid having to pay a gambling debt?

But the high drama of the court case continued. Statements now confirmed that the excess strychnine had indeed been handed to Morgan after the animals were killed. But the heat was oppressive during the trial, and on one occasion the alcoholism had kept Morgan in his cell in Lincoln. But the witnesses eventually came forward, one woman fainting in the heat as Mr Page, representing the accused, vainly attempted to explain the nature of his client.

The last but not the least piece of interest in this murder was the extreme difficulty involved in having Morgan brought to court from Lincoln prison. Some kind of defence should have been put together because it emerged that Morgan was in the habit of taking very small amounts of strychnine in a 'pick me up' mixture he had. His possession of the substance would thus have been made a matter of routine. But everything was further delayed when an officious chief warder wrote a 'jobsworth' letter explaining that he could not release Morgan for appearance in court: 'Prisoner cannot be released except on *habeas corpus* or on Secretary of State's order.'

But all was cleared up eventually and Morgan avoided the rope. There was uncertainty about premeditation, so he was given a long sentence. Several local journalists made their name from the case, and public interest was intense and prolonged. The appearance of Morgan was anticipated with the glamour and sensation more appropriate to the status of a celebrity, and for a short time, so he was.

CHAPTER 16

A Fight in the School Room
1892

Poor Ralphs shouted for the boys to help him, and this led to the unseemly sight of a crowd of boys pulling their churchman off, as you would a rabid dog in a fight.

Sometimes a confrontation with violent intent is a foul deed and little else: a matter of instant enmity or the culmination of a long rankling hatred. But, at times, history throws up a story that, while it has extreme violence, also has a streak of the bizarre running through it.

Such is the case of a rough and hot-tempered fight that took place in a small village schoolroom. North Kelsey in the last decade of the nineteenth century was a tiny place. Even today, it is a small village, just a few miles south of Brigg. But the size of a place is no guarantee that things will not get out of hand. They did just that one day in 1892 when the vicar, the Reverend Curry, set about the schoolmaster, Mr Ralphs, actually in the school classroom, and in front of the pupils. The local journalist had to admit that he felt 'deeply pained' at this particular scrap. But this was no light show of temper and a tantrum. In modern terms, it was an explosion of stress-related feelings, but there was also a deep aggression underneath.

As with most serious assaults, the catalyst does not seem significant when we look with hindsight. Mr Ralphs had been allowed to have a school photograph taken, with permission of the School Board. But this was the last thing that Curry was going to allow on this fateful day. He spoke to the letter of the law and insisted that in his capacity as Vicar he could give the orders until mid-morning. Ralphs' response was to aim to take the children out onto the road for the picture, and this was the spark that ignited the row.

The class were commanded to stay where they were. The vicar was then pushed into action when, after bolting one door and saying that none should leave the room, Ralphs opened another door and that was the final straw. Curry leapt across the room, slammed the door on the poor man's arm, and then held him fast. Poor Ralphs shouted for the boys to help him, and this led to the unseemly sight of a crowd of boys pulling their churchman off, as you would a rabid dog in a fight.

When the door was opened and the boys let go, Curry was still not finished; he grabbed the teacher and swung him round, thumping his body heavily against a wall and then onto some desks. This led to the climax, as the vicar chased after the teacher and took him by the throat, digging in his knuckles and seizing him in a tight hold. The children were taking the opportunity to escape, and when Ralphs wrestled free, he led the last few scholars out into the road, leaving Curry inside.

The amazing fact about the relationship at the basis of the fracas is that Ralphs had been teaching there for six years, and on a voluntary basis. It appears that, as Ralphs was teaching religious education, there was a difference of opinion somewhere, either on teaching methods or on dogma. Ralphs' arm was severely injured, yet at the hearing (informal, before action was decided on) the vicar claimed he had never seen the teacher's arm across the doorway. Either he was in a crazy rage or something close to envy and spite had driven him to act after years of enmity.

There is a very modern feel to the consequences: the National Union of Elementary Teachers took up the case and it went to the courts. Curry was not punished, and we would use the phrase 'it all blew over.' A personality defect was at the core. But the matter did not end there. A heated correspondence followed, and it is clear that the vicar was well-liked by his parishioners. 'A Churchman' sprang to his defence a week after, and wrote that this was another case of attacking the feudal spirit. He said, 'There are villages where the squire still exercises his autocratic will...Has the reverend Vicar of North Kelsey no defence? Is this another case of clerical oppression?' The man had been dismayed that the story had not been developed more in the intervening two days since the assault.

Unfortunately for the moral issue at the heart of the events, it was local election time the next week, and the violence was useful to certain conservative factions. What no-one at the time thought worthy of mention is what might have been put in the minds of the children as they witnessed this?

The research of local historian, A J Kerswill has unearthed more details about the vicar. There had been a small school built on the moor in 1872, with a cottage for the teacher, but there had been difficulties in finding any staff, despite Reverend Curry's attempts to find 'A mistress ... who must be willing to sit for a certificate.' He wanted 'A married woman whose husband would work in the neighbourhood.' But by 1882 a school inspector, Mr J Wilson, wrote to Curry to ask why the school had been discontinued. He noted that when he had been there last he heard 'one girl of about twelve saying that she had not been to school for three years.'

It is not difficult to see why there had always been problems accommodating the children of North Kelsey in a schoolroom during Reverend Curry's time there. If the clergyman had been charged, he would undoubtedly have appeared before a Consistory Court in Lincoln, as the recent Clergy Discipline Act of this same year would have meant that internal matters within the church would have been dealt with by the Bishop. A few years later, in 1904, a vicar from Carrington was defrocked by this process, but that had been for a sexual misdemeanour.

CHAPTER 17

Broughton Attacks
1892
The woman wanted justice ...

Around Broughton and Brigg at the end of the Victorian period, there appears to have been a series of nasty and violent assaults, sometimes related to drink but not always so. In Brigg there had been an occasion when extra police were brought into the town to control mobs of lads out for trouble, and there had been a serious riot in the place when an Irishman was hit by a truncheon and all his friends were out to attack Peelers. The police were barricaded in the *Angel Hotel* for protection.

But there were several cases in which more severe trouble was evident, and one involved a man who had been a threat to women in Broughton for some time. This was one Alfred Taylor, and he was obviously a dangerous man. It seems hard to believe that he had escaped a prison sentence before the occurrence that finally led him into a serious crime.

The Angel Hotel, Brigg. The author

A comment at the time noted that Taylor was 'not altogether right' and this has to be a spectacular understatement. He followed a Mrs Taylor for a long distance, as she walked from Wressle House to Broughton. He had seen her in Brigg and decided to track her and attack her. As she reached a stretch of road near Castlethorpe, he moved right behind her and whispered threats, notably one she recalled clearly: 'I wish she'd tumble.' Those words clearly suggest a sexual motive, but he seems to have not gone beyond hitting her in the face. He lost his nerve and ran away towards Brigg, but not before he grabbed her dress and had another intention in his mind. When Mrs Taylor yelled out 'Murder' it did enough to deter him and he panicked.

The woman wanted justice, though, and that same night she returned with friends to Brigg and identified him. The police were called and Inspector Danby came to ask questions of the man. Luckily for Mrs Taylor there was a witness: Edward Whelpton was working in the fields that day and had seen Taylor on the road at the time given by the complainant.

What seems outrageous now is that Taylor, as the trial noted, had a track record of attacks on women and had indeed been found guilty. To make matters worse for him, he had run away to Barnsley and most likely hoped that the affair would 'blow over' and be forgotten. But he was wrong. He was sentenced to two months in prison and a fine of £2. 10s. or another month in prison. The impression made of Taylor is that he was a pathetic character who would try to do anything rather than pay for his errors; his mother pleaded for him, stressing the fact that he was a family man and had children; then Taylor himself begged to be allowed to simply pay cash rather than have a custodial sentence. None of this did him any good.

A strange parallel case at that time concerned a point of procedure; clearly drunk and disorderliness was a common offence, and Brigg has always been notable for its number and quality of ale-houses to cater for the casual agricultural labour clientele. But in one instance, an officer called Goodson had arrested a violent drunk and had not been able to obtain a corroborative witness. The simple fact was that decent and respectable people would not be around the streets and pubs late at night. The only option was for a constable to act alone.

Disorder in the streets was common at most times, but the chronicles of this area for the decade show that something about the time and place combined to make these villages quite dangerous places for people walking alone. There was violence always ready to erupt. A day before Mrs Taylor was attacked, a Welshman had been kicked and beaten in a saloon simply for his nationality. But Mr Pryce had not helped his cause by throwing a spittoon at one of his attackers.

It was a hard life for the farm labourer: long hours in the fields and a thirst to slake in the villages and market towns around Scunthorpe. This was surely a recipe for crime and sometimes serious trouble.

CHAPTER 18

Brutality to his Wife
1898

'I'll kill you, you bitch!'

One subject in the history of crime in Britain is particularly remarkable for how we register changing moral attitudes in family life: wife-beating. Scanning local newspapers and social history reference works reinforces the view that a century ago, in many communities, brutality against members of the family was not always punished, and was sometimes indeed ignored. There are even cases of families starving children in order to buy alcohol.

George Parker and his wife Sarah definitely liked a drink. They had a long history of violence towards each other, but at the beginning of this particular day in which Parker when so far that he committed a very serious assault on his wife, there were all the right circumstances for an explosive event in their home.

This took place in Market Street, Gainsborough, where they lived, he working as a paperhanger and she at home. There is a shadowy presence over the following brutal events, though. This is a certain character called R Walter Forrest who may well have been Sarah's lover and the cause of at least some of the trouble. The poor woman clearly needed someone to care for her: her husband wanted her dead. They had been married for eleven years and none of them appear to have been happy ones.

On the March morning that began this awful attack, George emerged from his bed fully clothed and yelled for Sarah to fetch in some beer. She did this, and he took the beer upstairs. This made his condition much worse. When he came down he was ready to kill. Luckily, Sarah had a woman-friend sitting with her downstairs, so there was a witness from the very start. This was Ada Shorthouse, who swore that she had heard Parker say, when he came down again, 'I'll kill you, you bitch!' Parker took Sarah

Market Street, Gainsborough. The author

upstairs and there was a row. Shorthouse must have kept out of the way and been frightened for her life as well as her friend's. Sarah was at first kicked and beaten about the face. When Ada knew that Parker was totally out of control and was trying to throttle his wife, she ran for a police officer.

Two policemen came and took hold of Parker; he then promised to behave, but, unbelievably, he kicked his wife again, in front of the officers. By this time, Ada's sister Edith had also come into the house, so there were two witnesses now. All swore that Sarah had been 'tipsy' all day, but one has to say that this is understandable. She had nine deep bruises on her when the doctor came.

When statements were finally made, it turned out that a few days before this, Edith Shorthouse had run upstairs to see what was the cause of the noise and screaming, to see Parker standing over his wife and whipping her. That night, Sarah had asked her friend Edith to stay and sleep with her, to protect her from the monster in the house.

Dr Farrar, who came on the day when things came to a head and the law intervened, insisted that Parker would do much more harm if he were not removed from the premises. He said, 'If the brute won't be quiet, take him in.' Parker was out of all reasonable behaviour; he had a severe drink problem, and was potentially a threat to anyone near him.

All this is a straightforward narrative, with a quite familiar scenario: the drink, the aggression, and a deep resentment or hatred, probably fuelled by the wife's affair with the mysterious Mr Forrest. Yet it is on record that Sarah had not been free from guilt in the arena: she had apparently several times assaulted her husband, and was almost always intoxicated. The story then seems close to the emotional turmoil of the play *Who's Afraid of Virginia Woolf* by Edward Albee: the archetypal mutual love-hate relationship. However, none of this erases the hard fact that on this day, Parker had the capability, the mind-set and the lack of control that could easily have led him to kill, and his wife Sarah was the weakest and most vulnerable person in his tempestuous orbit.

CHAPTER 19

The Murderer's Suicide Note
1901
'This I could not allow'

This is one of those stories that is intriguingly unresolved, and opens up more questions as more possibilities emerge.

It began when the builders were working on number 59, Wrawby Street in Brigg. As workmen took floorboards out, they found a cache of letters and one, separate from the rest, was on one sheet of paper, with a scribbled note in blue; this had been put in a sealed envelope, and had even been waxed. It was a suicide note. This was written on the sheet:

Sunday 4th day of August.
To whom it may concern.
I, Thomas Benjamin Swift, now and on this day of Sunday in the year of our Lord 1901, do hereby confess to the murder of Molly Brown, maid of this establishment. We had meetings, and she threatened to reveal that she had conceived. This I could not allow. Now I cannot live with the burden of guilt any longer so I have decided to end it all.

Whosoever should find this letter make all haste to the parish vicar so that he can pray for my forgiveness.

David Robinson, who first wrote about the note, comments that, in 1994, he searched the trade directories and found that the property was owned by one John Broughton, a grocer, in 1896. Then, by 1909 the tradesman there was Samuel Danby, a draper. David Robinson notes that other letters found in the cache referred to Molly Brown. But there are no records of any murder. The material presents us with a piece of detective work. There are several possibilities: the whole thing may be a hoax done much later, for some amusement; the letter may have been written at the time, but for similar reasons, or it may

59, Wrawby Street, where the note was found. The author

have been fabricated by a journalist for other writers to access. Of course, it may be perfectly genuine. One detail in support of this is the authenticity of the language. The phrase, 'This I could not allow' is convincing as the expression and tone of the time. The extreme formality of the note also suggests that there is a real feeling there, totally unbearable guilt.

Of course, the limited information given makes the murder, if there was one, something that took place any time between say 1870 and the late 1890s. The possibility is that the writer was not a young man at the time of writing, but was most likely a middle-aged man of some local respectability, and that point in time would fall largely within those years

Who was this man Swift? There are twenty Swifts listed in county records and indeed there is a Thomas Swift who died in 1901 (in March). This is the only candidate, and records have no statistic of a man called Swift who committed suicide.

Things begin to look more dubious when one considers that there are no available names in Coroners' reports for Glanford for the period covering the date itself and the two years succeeding (as there was often a delay in the writing after the death).

Holmsian deduction also raises questions about the fact that the letter was under a floorboard. There seems to be no reason for that, as it would make discovery more than likely in a far distant time in the future. If the determination for self-killing were so resolute, why do this and then mention the vicar? Such a reference implies that the man wanted the fact known in the community.

Detectives might also question the appearance of the note. The red sealing wax and the formality might suggest a too high degree of ritual and rather showy procedure: was a hoaxer trying too hard to create a false trail? It seems so. In the context of Lincolnshire, from Glanford down to Boston, there have been well-to-do families of Swifts, but the only (very slender) connection to this man would have been the Thomas Swift who died in Belton in 1901.

The questions go on and on. It seems that the affair is a trick. But there is one nagging detail – the vocabulary is so apposite for the time and place. The motive for the killing is also convincing, given the ethics of the time and the absolute centrality of local reputation for a man of means. Maybe in time other facts will emerge and we will know if we really have two interesting deaths here: a suicide and a murder.

CHAPTER 20

A Tragic Suicide, Brigg
1905

It had all been so clinically done: he had stood on a box, and when hanged, his feet were only just off the ground.

Taking one's own life was, until 1961, a crime, but in the period covering the Victorian and Edward years, the reasons for suicide usually throw up interesting and informative elements of social history: the plain fact is that an act of taking one's own life always highlights something in the immediate social context. This is often a case of 'something rotten in the state of Denmark' as Shakespeare's

Coney Court, Brigg. The author

Hamlet puts it. Some of the commonest reasons are logically concerned with the social consequences of some intolerable guilt or culpability for a particular wrong. Often, it is a case of disgrace, pure and simple. An individual has done something wrong and the consequences will be too hard to bear.

Yet in the sad case of the greengrocer, George Draper of Brigg, the cause was one that will unfortunately always be with us: he was in extreme debt. It must have been a terrible shock for John Neal, who found the body suspended from a halter in Draper's home in Coney Court. This was in a shed, and the man had double-tied a rope around his neck, with a handkerchief for a pad. Dr Goodman, who came to deal with the body, had known Draper for many years. He stated that there were no other marks of violence. The place was a dark and enclosed court off the town streets, a spot in which such an awful action would have been unnoticed and out of any public concourse at the time. He chose the place and time with the precise and clear thinking of someone determined to see it through to the end.

It had all been so clinically done: he had stood on a small box, and when hanged, his feet were only just off the ground. All Neal could say when asked to explain this horror was, 'He was in the habit of having a drop too much sometimes.' But Mrs Draper knew what was really at the heart of this tragedy. No-one had seen him since eight the previous night. But his wife had said that he had been feeling low all day and that they both knew that the time was approaching when he was to face his creditors. In fact, he was expecting a summons at Christmastime, just before the holiday.

George Draper had apparently been sober all day, but in the evening, he did talk to his wife of 'making away with' himself. She had naturally talked him down from this mental state and in fact torn a strip off him for such daft thoughts that would not solve anything.

On 6 January, the coroner said that in the previous year there had been forty-nine inquests and over half of these had involved violent deaths. With this sad suicide in mind, and the general level of offences against the person, there was a long and heated correspondence in the local newspaper at the time of Draper's death, asking the question, 'Has the Devil Captured Brigg?' The letters began to wander from the general drunkenness and violence to such topics as whether or not specific religious persons in the area had been capable of 'noble self-sacrifice' for goodness and right-thinking.

The year 1905 was not a good one for Lincolnshire in respect of self-harm. The most plaintive and melancholy case was a few days after Draper's downfall in Lincoln, when a married woman called Harriet Lynn was found dead on the racecourse with a suicide note by her; again, oddly, her death was an unusual suicide, that barely relates to any social trend: she said simply, 'I am not fit to live with you. I took some aromatic ginger and it caused me all this trouble. I hope you will forgive me for this awful deed but it is too late now.'

It was in truth a year of living dangerously, and George Draper and Harriet Lynn's stories evoke intensely personal stories for which we will never have a full explanation. A comment made about Draper by a neighbour states the continuing bafflement we feel when such a thing occurs: 'He was always genial. He has never been heard to talk of suicide or doing this sort of lamentable act. It is puzzling in the extreme to contemplate this death in a small community.'

CHAPTER 21

The Brute of Manley Street
1911

... nothing can excuse the savagery of
William Rylatt.

Manley Street today is very close to the newly developed centre of Scunthorpe, close to The Parishes and the library and film theatre. To walk there today is to see only buses and asphalt parking. It is hard to imagine what this part of town was like in the early years of the twentieth century, but one thing is certain: it was a cramped place, with working families living on top of each other. Work was long and hard and took its toll on men and women then. Many men who wandered onto the wrong side of the law might give excuses about their bad tempers and exhaustion after a long shift, but nothing can excuse the savagery of William Rylatt.

Worse still, the brute turned his rancour and violence on his young wife. Not that he was one of the men working hard at any trade; he didn't do much at all except drink and use his fists. He was in the habit of hitting Sarah, and seems to have built this habit into their lifestyle for a while, until one day it all got out of hand.

One morning, she prepared her brother's breakfast and then felt faint, so she went back to bed. Her daughter very kindly brought her some tea, but from that point, Rylatt snapped: he spat in the tea after following the girl upstairs, clearly on the edge. His nerves frayed. The next stage was to grab his wife by the hair and shove her hard against the bedroom wall. As if this was not enough suffering for the poor woman, he then dragged her around the house, holding her roughly by her hair. She screamed in pain. The noise was so extreme that a neighbour came in to intervene, and luckily a builder called Charles Lockwood, who later testified that these kinds of

Manley Street now, after recent re-development. The author

things had been happening for some time, took control of the situation at the time, and eventually, on recovery, Sarah went to the police station.

Lockwood said that there had been two years of such abuse, but never as severe as this episode. For his part, Rylatt admitted just to some of the nasty behaviour, but not all. What came out at the trial was yet another story of his violence, and this had happened on the wedding day of his niece. The couple had come home and found her waiting up for him. He pushed her off a stool and hit her. From that point she had been afraid to live with him and lived in abject terror. It took the explosion of emotions that led to the neighbours coming into the house to make something actually happen to help the wife.

At the trial, Dr Reid said that Sarah was badly bruised and in a state of severe shock when he came to her; the crowd gathered to rightly vilify the culprit. A Mrs Lounds said that Rylatt was 'a cruel monster' and his step-daughter, Jenny

Manley Street as shown on the 1906 Ordnance Survey map.

Clark, testified that he was 'a complete animal.' The good builder Lockwood, summed it up well: 'I had to step in that night to stop the man thrashing his wife to her death ...'

There were some quieter days at number 51 Manley Street for a long time after that. Rylatt had a long spell in prison. But, as with so many of these domestic brutality cases, history loses track of the participants in the drama, and only rarely is the final outcome of such cruel relationships ever known. We have to hope that William Rylatt either changed his ways or changed his address and left the woman he had tortured for so long with a new life – a peaceful one.

CHAPTER 22

Murder Talk in the *Talbot*
1919

... his only defence was that there was mental illness in the family.

Crimes of passion vary so much in their nature and in the surrounding circumstances, that it is always hard to differentiate between the justness of a kind of thoughtless and spontaneous action against a loved one, and a planned assault. The details of evidence given by witnesses, as well as biographical factors, are always important. In this case, there was no problem in deciding on the circumstances leading to the murder of a beloved by the lover. That this happened in the quiet market town of Caistor is all the more surprising, but then, there has always been serious crime wherever emotions exist in dangerous and extreme forms.

William Wright sat in the *Talbot* public house in Caistor on 28 October 1919 and muttered the words, 'Murder, black cap, three weeks, hanged by the neck, finished.' It was very odd behaviour. But the words proved true almost to the letter. His crime was that he strangled his sweetheart, Annie Coulbeck, with a scarf. Annie was pregnant with Wright's child at the time. He had walked into her home at Pigeon Spring, Horse Market, and killed her, apparently over a brooch she was wearing.

The words spoken in the hotel were spoken because his sweetheart was being discussed by the people with him. Later that night he went to her at ten o'clock and the killing was done shortly after that. He had seen a lot of life, having been in the army; and he had also been a tailor. But there was not much of his life left after that night.

Annie's body was discovered the next morning by a neighbour. The door was open, and there she was, dead on the floor. She must have still had the brooch that was the cause of

Wright's irrational jealousy. That seems to have been the reason for the murder; Annie had told Wright that the brooch was given to her by her mother, but he had been convinced that she was lying, and that she had a lover. His statement, made later in court, was that after speaking about the jewellery, he strangled her, then went home after very blandly putting out the lamp.

Of course he was soon picked up by the police, and his only defence was that there was mental illness in his family. The question was, did the man commit a premeditated murder and was he of sound mind? Defence talked about the fact that Wright's mother had been placed in an asylum the previous year, and that other members of his family had various illnesses, such as his sister who had a religious mania, and an uncle who had been in Lincoln County Asylum, and had in fact died while incarcerated there. Had there been any real substance in this line of thought as a defence ploy, there would have had to have been ample evidence that Wright's condition was constant and profound, not something emerging on that specific day with that self-generated provocation. It was a crime in the *Othello* mould, but without the grandiose stature of that tragic hero.

But none of this was to any effect; the truth was that he had spoken of murder shortly before going to kill Annie. He was aware of what he was doing at the time, and witnesses heard him speak the words in the *Talbot*. There was an appeal, but it was easily dismissed, and his fate was sealed. Wright talked to the prison chaplain about the day of the murder, and at last stated openly that he had intended to do it. He knew that the punishment was just. The reporter writing for a local newspaper noted that, 'As far as is known he showed no repentance for his foul deed.'

Mr Justice Horridge did indeed wear the black cap and all the efforts of defence counsel Emery were to no avail. The man's prophecy had been correct in every detail, apart from the fact that he died five weeks after the trial, not three weeks.

There is considerable detail recorded about his death at the hands of Henry Pierrepoint at Lincoln gaol in 1920. Wright was cool; he gave no struggle when he was pinioned, and it took only thirty seconds for him to die after stepping from the condemned cell. It had been thirteen years since there had been an execution in Lincoln.

CHAPTER **23**

Death Sentence for a Teenager
Waddingham, 1931
... just a quiet murmur of 'amen' from the chaplain.

Waddingham, a village only eight miles from Scunthorpe, became the focus of a national debate in 1931, and the reason for this was that Harold Smith, just sixteen-years-old, had murdered his aunt in the bedroom of isolated Holmes Farm. At that time, no-one so young had been executed in Britain for forty years; but Justice MacKinnon had donned his black cap and passed the death sentence on the boy in Lincoln, with just a quiet murmur of 'amen' from the chaplain.

The killings had indeed been horrific: Anne and Robert Jacklin were found dead in their bed by Robert's father, who had visited one morning and found himself faced first of all by a fire smouldering downstairs, where some hay had been lit, and then hearing the cries of his grand-child upstairs: this was before he walked into the bedroom and saw the body of his daughter-in-law and then his son, still alive, covered in blood. He had had to force his way in after hearing no response to his shouts.

Robert survived for two days, before dying in the Lincoln County hospital. His upper jaw and nose had been shot away. His only recorded account of the incident as he lay dying in agony, was that he had woken up to find his wife covered in blood and that he had no explanation for what had taken place in his lonely farmhouse.

Young Smith had told two stories. The first was that he had decided, after simply not being 'able to get on' with his aunt and uncle, who employed him, that he had had enough and he was going to shoot them. He said that he picked up a shotgun and then stood at their bedroom door for a while, deciding whether or not to actually kill them. He knew they were both in bed. 'I got out of bed about quarter past four, got the shotgun and stood outside the bedroom for four or five minutes.'

His second statement was that his uncle Robert had shot his aunt and then turned the gun on himself. A medical expert confirmed that the suicide of Robert Jacklin was quite plausible, as the wounds were consistent with

Robert Jacklin talks to D S Dolby. Laura Carter

a shot fired from close range. This seemed like a bizarre theory; the implication was that a strange account was put to the jury: one which said that Jacklin had seen his wife dead, just as he woke up, and then, in sheer despair, found a gun and shot himself through the jaw. The whole idea was ridiculous.

So who shot the husband? Nothing is clear on that point. All that was to happen related solely to the murder of Annie Jacklin, and the finger pointed to Harold Smith. He was found guilty of murder but with a strong recommendation for mercy. But the death sentence was passed, and the papers reported that the young man had been remarkably calm in the dock on

Scene of the crime, farm house at Waddingham. 'X' marks the spot. Laura Carter

that occasion: 'he remained calm and showed no traces of emotion.' Journalists went away to search for facts about the last hangings of teenagers, and noted that five people of eighteen years of age had been executed in the years since 1885. There were discussions in the press about the need for law reform on this matter for some time.

The Home Secretary, Sir Herbert Samuel, was appealed to; popular opinion insisted that the whole matter needed clearing up, and that Samuel was the man to do it. One of the prominent lawyers in the debate expressed the dilemma in this way: 'I am sure that public opinion cannot approve of the death sentence being passed on boys of this tender age when there is no likelihood of it being carried into effect.'

The sentence was commuted to penal servitude. This was the sentence that had been brought in as long ago as 1853, as it was being realised just how expensive transportation to Australia was – and also how perilous to the health of convicts. Smith was destined to be breaking rocks and sewing mailbags for his entire life.

The tale is surely an important milestone in the long and contentious development of more humane sentencing in the British prison system, and also testifies to the still largely unchanged nature of penal ideas in the inter-war years.

The nagging doubt is about the nature of the two gunshot wounds. The fact is that both appear to have been from close

range. This may still indicate that Harold killed his aunt, but that he advanced and came close to her before firing. There is still a possibility that he did the same to his uncle, and this seems far more likely than the bizarre suicide theory. The fact remains that we will never really know precisely how Robert Jacklin died. But the sorry tale was one of high drama: there was blood running down the walls of the cottage when Robert's father came. That would hint that Robert had perhaps run to a window to call for help.

Justice MacKinnon. Laura Carter

Young Smith was not at the scene when old James Jacklin came and made the grisly discovery; the boy had run away in fear. The tale behind that fact could either be that he had shot them both but ran in terror on seeing that his uncle was still alive and was staggering to the window, or equally that he had come across the scene of murder and been horrified that he might be next.

Sir H Samuel. Laura Carter

Harold from Scawby Brook had certainly made the headlines, but for the wrong reasons. The fact that he told two stories went against him in the end, naturally, and from that fact stems most of the doubt and confusion.

CHAPTER 24

An Attack in Ashby
1938

*... very drunk and aggressive in Morley Street
after a Saturday night binge.*

In British social history, particularly since the early years of the nineteenth century, there has been, until the first decades of the twentieth century, a degree of antipathy between the police and Irish immigrants. A public house in Leeds in the 1840s had a notice over a table saying, 'No swaddy Irish or soldiers wanted here.' After the Famine, in 1847, around a quarter of a million Irish people came to Britain via Liverpool. Many of these people went to the Midlands, and of course, to Lincolnshire, a place known for potato crops.

In the *Punch* cartoons of Victorian England, and in the writings of Henry Mayhew in the middle years of the nineteenth century, the popular stereotype of the brawling Irishman on the wrong side of the law is everywhere. Mayhew talks about them in this way: 'I've known wild Irishmen get into the wards with knives and sticks hidden about their persons, to be ready for a fight.' The fact is that there is a massive body of writing about what Friedrich Engels called 'the volatile, dissolute and drunken Irish' and it has to be remembered that there was a considerable amount of xenophobia in the English working man at that time – and some anti-Catholic feeling.

But the occasion of a violent confrontation involving Irish workers has always made the news pages, and Scunthorpe has had its share. In 1938 there was one cluster of street violence involving Irish workers and drink that ended with a prison sentence. The inter-war years had been a period of expansion for the town, and two new blast furnaces had been built, and Appleby steelworks came into operation in 1927. All this needed cheap labour. The chain of working shifts, heavy drinking and crime shifted into top gear. There was clearly a large problem with violent street crime in the 1930s.

The main culprit in this case was Dennis Kelly, a homeless man who was very drunk and aggressive in Morley Street after a Saturday night binge. He found his way to a fish shop, and there he was so out of control that the police were sent for and Inspector Cook arrived to bring him out of the premises. Then the attack began. Kelly struck and kicked the Inspector, and eventually threw himself on the ground. The only statement he was able to make was that he had drunk several whiskies.

The second Irish fighter was Daniel Doherty, a man who foolishly mixed medicines with spirit-drinking and went out looking for trouble. He chose Brigg Road as his arena and after provoking a brawl, was taken into custody. A cell would have been welcome; like Kelly, he had no fixed abode. But we are not finished yet.

Alexandra Road, Ashby. The author

Poor Inspector Cook, on this fateful day, was yet to meet two more men who wanted trouble. Another Kelly (Patrick) managed to avoid striking the poor policeman, but eventually, after using his fists a deal, was hit by a motor vehicle and he was silenced. But this Saturday in February, 1938 still had a certain Frederick Speed, but not an Irishman. Speed went into a fit of cursing and violence so extreme that first, near his home in Alexandra Road, Ashby, as he rode a bike, and then when arrested, he attacked the law officer and had to be handcuffed. Inspector Cook had had a busy day.

The Chairman of the Bench, Mr Nixon, clearly had the unfortunate detective in mind when he said that he could not overlook the assault on the officer of the law, and that a custodial sentence on Kelly was necessary. He received two short concurrent prison sentences.

These offences are typical of the period and the place; casual labour was arriving in the area both for labouring in the steel industry and for casual farm labour up the road in Brigg and Scawby areas. Farmlands on the Trentside had also been improved steadily since the 1850s, and always needed extra labour.

At the time this very visible and alarming fracas took place in the streets of Scunthorpe, J B Priestley was writing of the Irish immigrants in Liverpool, 'The Irishman in Ireland may be the…. best fellow in the world. But the Irishman in England too often cuts a very miserable figure.' There were some miserable figures in the Scunthorpe police cells that Saturday night in February over seventy years ago.

CHAPTER 25

The Black-Out Terror
1940–41

'Something happened to me, and I have no control over myself.'

History does not really associate Scunthorpe with the black-out experience of the Second World War. It is curious that the town was not a primary target of the bombers, when they bombarded nearby Hull so mercilessly. There was a story that the steelworks had managed to cover up the molten metal glow, and, as Nick Lyons has said, this is 'gross nonsense' as the RAF Bomber crews used the glow from the steelworks as an important geographical marker on their home run.

But the dark nights brought another kind of terror to the town: this one in the shape of a man who preyed on defenceless young women. For several weeks in the early months of 1941 and in late 1940 he attacked and robbed several women. It was a piece of excellent detective work, stemming from sheer acute observation of detail, that caught him. The first headline in the local newspaper was 'Convoys to Defeat Scunthorpe Terror.' That was no exaggeration; it was a frightening time.

The 'convoy' system was quite simply that women would not walk out alone. During the reign of terror, Thomas Horstead, only twenty-one years of age, attacked and robbed three women, one of them actually in her own home. The climate of fear lasted for three months.

First he had robbed Joan Tattersall. His assault had been very violent, to the extent that he had tried to choke her. Then he pinpointed Mrs Olive Robinson and this involved a struggle, as she put up a fight. At the trial before Justice MacNaughten in Nottingham, Mrs Robinson said that Horstead walked past her, and as he did so he struck her across the left side of her face. This blow knocked her to the ground, but she managed to get to her feet and tackle him. She hit him several times, and there was a prolonged struggle, before he took her bag and hopped away over a nearby fence.

The turning point came when the young villain crept into the home of Mrs Vera Moody on 3 December 1940. She reported that she had heard a sound, as she was in the house with only her baby for company (her husband was away in the army); then she went to confront him, and saw him holding onto the door. She knocked frantically on the wall to alert her neighbours but there was no response. Vera ran for her life, going to the nearest warden post. But she had noticed a detail that would lead to his capture: on his hand was a yellow strip of plaster.

The man took Vera's handbag, but she told the police, of course. Now, D S Montgomery had seen this yellow plaster and recalled the man. When Horstead went home with his booty, the detective was waiting for him, and the game was up. At the time, the man had told police that he remembered the Tattersall attack and that he had attacked her: 'When I attacked her she fell down and, in order to get her handbag, I had to pull her away by the legs. I hid the handbag in a front garden in Buckingham Street.'

What was emerging, moreover, was that his attacks had a sexual element also. When he seized Joan Tattersall he had grabbed her around the neck, and her words describing what happened next convey the fact that he committed an indecent assault on her: 'He put his arm around my neck from behind' she stated. Joan was only sixteen-years-old, walking home in the dark.

At the first hearing, sentence was postponed because of the sexual aspect of the case. At Lincoln Assizes, Mr Justice MacNaughten was troubled by the nature of the indecent assault and asked that the prisoner be observed before the full trial in Nottingham. Horstead had a record; he had been at Lindsey Quarter Sessions for nine counts of house-breaking and also charges of larceny. He was moving on to bolder crimes and enjoying it. In his own words, he said, after first revelling in the fact that he had kept out of trouble for nine months, 'Something happens to me, and I have no control over myself.'

Dr Norris, at the Lincoln hearing, said that the defendant was not mentally ill. A dramatic interchange took place between judge and medical man:

MacNaughten: 'Is he fit to receive corporal punishment?'

Dr Norris: 'Yes.'

More information came out about Horstead at Nottingham. He was a crane driver, and as he was on the steelworks, he was in a reserved occupation. He earned good money: £4. 18 shillings a week, and he was from a good home. When arrested he had said, 'I only do these things for excitement and on the spur of the moment' – as if that was some kind of defence.

Finally, before the sentence of six years penal servitude was passed, the judge had asked the doctor, who had been observing the prisoner in Lincoln gaol, if there was any evidence of insanity. The answer was no. The only explanation given was that he seemed to be suffering from some trouble he could not explain. Mr Smith, for the defence, had noted that the young man 'took a kind of glee' in his crimes. It seems clear, reading between the lines at the trial, that the judge

By the old bus station – a regular haunt of the 'Terror'. The author

wanted to apply some physical punishment, which he could have done, but he stated that, as there was no 'extreme sexual motive' that corporal punishment was undesirable. His final comment was, 'If it were possible to aggravate the gravity of your offence, I would do so' He meant, apply corporal punishment. On the last day of the affair, 26 February, Horstead started his six years of hard labour. So ended one of the most intense and dramatic episodes in the history of crime in Scunthorpe. The reign of terror had ended, and women could walk without fear on an evening, black-out or not.

CHAPTER 26

The Neighbour Thief
1941

The two families were in the habit of helping each other out in times of need.

This is a story that casts a shadow across the platitudes about the war years being a time when life was all about trust, community and the possibility of even leaving your door unlocked without fear of crime. In fact, this is a tale of neighbourliness gone wrong, as temptation came into the path of a woman who, on the surface was a typical 'good neighbour.' But the case of Linda Blythe also highlights another outcome of crimes committed in this community context: the notion of a *bona fide* entry into property rather than day-time house-breaking. Which was it to be? The issue kept the lawyers busy for some time.

In the wartime neighbourhood of Crosby, the Blythes and their next-door neighbours, the Goodyears, were clearly very close. Walls then were thin. Adults, children and pets often became the centre of mutual care and responsibility. The two families were in the habit of helping each other out in times of need. Yet there is a puzzle in this case: Mrs Goodyear was sure that her door could be opened by Linda Blythe's key, but she was not sure about the case vice versa. This is because Linda was in the habit of popping in to attend to the dog from time to time.

Now, on Boxing Day, 1941, the Goodyears said they were going out for the day, and Linda was heard to ask them where they were going and for how long. Mr Goodyear tended to leave his wallet at home, in a case, and sometimes locked in a kitchen cupboard. On this occasion, the latter was the case. Linda Blythe, at about two in the afternoon, came in through the back door. What she had not realised is that the daughter of the Goodyears, Doreen, was still at home, with the dog. Doreen walked through to the kitchen and saw Linda Blythe opening the cupboard. When the girl asked her what she was doing she said, 'I don't know. I don't know what I have done it for. I hope this will not make any difference to me and your mother.'

It obviously did make a difference. The wallet, which had contained almost £20 in notes, now had, Mr Goodyear said, £4 missing. There seems to have been some problem with Linda Blythe. Maybe she was suffering from extreme mental pressures. All that is clear is that she went to D C Evinson and asked for help; at that point she said she had given in to temptation, but on 14 January, she denied all knowledge of the money and the wallet. It was this that led to the case going to court.

In court Linda said, 'If it had not been for my family I would have admitted it before', and her attempts to placate the Goodyears had failed. She had approached Mr Goodyear and offered to 'pay some back on Friday and some more the week after.' But it was to no avail.

The legal wrangling was centred on whether or not Linda Blythe had a *bone fide* custom of entry into the home of her neighbour. The case for the defence made much of this. To complicate matters further, a claim now was made that the Goodyears' dog had been howling, and had indeed done so in the past; at such times Linda Blythe came in to attend to the animal. Therefore there was an element of good intention and in fact, actual assistance and concern here.

Nevertheless, the basic fact was that there had been a theft. What made the Goodyears' case a little fragile was that Mr Goodyear had said that £4 were missing , but admitted he was guessing and not certain what, if anything, had been taken. The *bone fide* entry was denied by the judge. Linda Blythe escaped a custodial sentence, and it was clear that keys were never exchanged again. Good neighbourliness faded away, too, after this. The incident highlighted the common custom of reliance on neighbours for help in small everyday matters; it also shone a torch of contention in that dark area of trust and co-operation so urgently needed in a community when the world around was at war and bombers were droning over the Humber estuary.

CHAPTER 27

Unexplained Death of a Doctor
1948

... there was something not quite right about his general health.

There are few things in law so frustrating as an open verdict, and when the cause of death is clearly some kind of poison, then the lack of a closure to the case is even more unsatisfactory. In the death of Dr Howard Lillie of Winterton, there is a yet even more remarkable factor: one of the drugs in his body was a mystery then and remains so now. As Katherine Wilson has shown in her recent work on poisoners and poisoning, *Poisoned Lives* (2004), until recent years, a death involving a poison has always had the muddle of several possibilities.

First, there is the option of a murder. Some persons unknown administer a poisonous substance; then there is the suicide question. Medical men are in a good position to know the effects of whatever substance they choose as the instrument of their demise. Finally, there is the distinct possibility of accidental death, even for a doctor. In certain circumstances, even the doctors take the wrong quantity, or create the wrong 'cocktail' for their body to take.

Around Christmas, 1947, Dr Lillie's wife found his body in bed. This was in King Street, Winterton, a quiet village to the east of Scunthorpe, on the Barton road. The first inquest, on 5 January, had been adjourned to allow time for further tests, but there was nothing decided a few weeks later, when the coroner, Eric Dyson, stated that 'He would much rather find some definite cause of death' but he was afraid that he could not. Even the Home Office Forensic Science Laboratory in Nottingham had been unable to offer a theory of cause of death.

Dr Lillie had served in the RAF from 1939 to the end of the war, and then he was invalided out, following a lung injury

King Street, Winterton. The author

sustained after being shot down over Africa. Since 1946 he
had never been well, suffering from asthma, and also having
periods of pneumonia. On the first day of the New Year he had
woken up early in the morning after only a few hours sleep but
said he was well; his wife was worried because he had been
most unwell the week earlier. Obviously, there was something
not quite right about his general health.

Some of the reasons for this began to appear when the
coroner, together with Dr Baldwin, area pathologist for
Lincoln, gave statements about their post-mortem
examinations. Their conclusions were mixed, and
inconclusive, there being no certainty about the actual cause
of death. There were, they said, traces of 'various drugs ' in the
corpse. Nothing was specified initially. But at that point a fact
emerged that may be the most enlightening detail in the story
of this mysterious death. Dr Lillie had been taking a drug
called emetine and Dr O'Reardon, his locum, made the point

that emetine was widely used in the Far East, principally for the treatment of dysentery. He noted that is was very rare to find anyone using the drug in Britain.

'Emetine' – this is logically some variety of drug working as an emetic: that is, causing vomiting. The fact is that Dr Lillie had very large amounts of the stuff in his surgery and the locum said that there were four phials of the drug as a rule, but that some of this had gone missing. Though everyone agreed that this was a very dangerous drug to have around, confoundingly, none of it was found in the body. This is odd, because the obvious conclusion with this drug in mind is that the doctor wanted to end his suffering. But, despite its presence, it did not figure in the death.

The last point made at the inquest was by Mr Hett, who was acting for Mrs Lillie. He asked Dr Baldwin the question any layman would like to ask in this situation: could a person die of 'natural causes' and yet no specific cause ever be found? The answer was a definite yes. There is no reason to think that there was any foul play. No-one had any motive to kill him. In the end, we turn to the realms of crime fiction here, as Agatha Christie did when using her knowledge of poisons, finding one that left no trace after death, in her novel, *The White Horse*. But there is nothing so dramatic or sensational in the case of the Winterton doctor. Most of the threadbare facts available hint at suicide.

CHAPTER 28

Murder on Queensway
1948

Joan was lying, her face in a pool of blood, still wearing her school uniform ...

This is a story of last-minute reprieve, the killer who almost went to the gallows being a housekeeper. She had committed a brutal murder, had the first appeal turned down, and then, with factors of 'unsound mind' and what we would now call stress and 'personal factors' impinging on the loss of control, Hilda Green was allowed to live on. Her crime had shaken the people of Ashby and the Queensway area in which the Mason family lived just after the Second World War.

When Mrs Crowston, living on the edge of Queensway, opened her door to her neighbour, steelworker Harold Mason, in December 1948, he told her that someone had killed his daughter Joan. Fourteen-years-old Joan Mason had been savagely attacked and left to die by her bicycle, only a short distance from her home in Clarkson House. Her father had been searching for her extensively, and finally came across her body in the moonlight.

She had last been seen cycling homewards from Ashby Girls School, and that sighting had been in Stockshill Road. This is not far from the busy Queensway trunk road that cuts through the suburbs of Scunthorpe, being part of the direct routes to Doncaster and to Lincoln. It is always busy, as it is also the main route to the steelworks.

Mr Mason was a widower. He was clearly very shocked as he reported the terrible scene to his neighbour. Joan was lying, her face in a pool of blood, still wearing her school uniform of a brown blazer, white blouse and grey gym-slip. She also had a double-breasted patterned coat, but that was missing from the scene of the crime. At the time, reporters described her as well-built and that despite her robustness, someone had

The area around Clarkson House, Ashby, by Queensway. The author

attacked her with great force and she had been unable to resist. She had been killed some hours before being found. The date was 15 December, and she had been meaning to ride into Scunthorpe to do some Christmas shopping.

The first report stressed the position of her home: noting that the Masons lived in a place facing the 'growing aluminium pre-fab estate across the busy Grimsby-Doncaster Road', and made the point that no 'morbid' crowd had gathered. Yet there was a high presence of police staff, and a search began; a pathologist came from Peterborough, and optimistically, there were 'certain clues' recorded.

The Masons had lived in Clarkson House for twelve years, and a neighbour said that Mr Mason had been 'mother and father to Joan' after Mrs Mason's death five years previously. On her part, Joan was a good little housekeeper, and her aunt told reporters that her usual practice was to go home and prepare a meal for her father, as well as house-keeping. She had talked of staying home to look after her father when she reached the age of fifteen. She was clearly well liked, and locals called her a 'lovable little girl'. There were plenty of relatives to be shocked – and it was a shocking killing.

On the next day the coat was still missing, but at the inquest, Mr Mason gave a more detailed account of events, and spoke sadly of the last time he saw his daughter, lying in bed on the morning of the attack. He had worked the 7.30 to 4.30 shift at Appleby-Frodingham The focus of enquiry was on the home – Clarkson House itself and this was significant. Mason had spoken of Joan sleeping in a separate room, but that there was also a housekeeper in the home. Mr Mason was a man of regular habits; he spoke of putting his bike in a former air-raid shelter, and also of putting an alarm clock in his daughter's room before he left for work. Plaintively, he said that on his arrival home he did not see a light, as he usually did.

The only person he found in the home at this point at which routine was broken, was housekeeper, Hilda Green. But the search among neighbours went on, including a Mr Ullyat who saw Mason looking desperately for his daughter. The police enquiry extended to the point of appealing to motorists. D I Swann and others spoke to motorists and other passers-by, as the night of the killing had been a full moon and the officers were hopeful of a lead. George Price of the Forensic Science Laboratory in Nottingham was also involved, and most work was still directed to the interior of the house.

Soon after this, the most significant development was made and D S Knowler talked about forensic work leading to a positive line of thought regarding the murder. It was only a matter of days before Hilda Green was arrested and charged. One of the notable aspects of this case was that Green's remand was constantly extended. In January 1949, her lawyer, H M Winocour, complained about the delays caused by the Director of Public Prosecutions. As he said, 'This is the third occasion on which she has been brought before a court.' This circumstance may well have been a factor in her reprieve, as she had to travel from Manchester for each hearing, and in Winocour's opinion, this entailed 'mental anguish.' At his third hearing, she smiled as she entered court. There was a strong public presence, principally 'about fifty women, housewives with shopping baskets' as the *Evening Telegraph* pointed out.

She was tried and sentenced to death, the hanging fixed for 9 April 1949 at Strangeways, but by 31 March the Home Secretary had reviewed the case. Green's appeal had been dismissed the week before, but now the final decision was a reprieve.

CHAPTER 29

Robbery with Violence, Laughton 1953

He was far too dangerous to be allowed to walk the streets of Scunthorpe.

Something made me go funny and the next thing I remember was that the woman was outside the van with blood on her face'. This was the explanation given by Reginald Percy Stowe, twenty-nine, of Ashby, after attacking Mrs Norah Wraith of Laughton, with a hammer. P C Dixon recalled the words with disbelief. He told Gainsborough magistrates that he had set about the forty-year-old woman on Thursday, 23 April, and left her bleeding on the roadside.

Stowe was a man of no character: nothing remarkable. He was a man whose habits and past gave no clue as to any possible source of such atrocious behaviour. The motive was as puzzling as that of Horstead in the black-out terror.

In the modern world, there would be a whole process of enquiry, and there would certainly be some investigation of all the possible factors in the man's life such as stress or even some kind of mental illness. As it happened, his eventual defence could muster nothing substantial. The incident goes down on record as one of those mysterious aberrations the human mind is subject to.

There is an interesting pattern in what can only be called a crime wave of offences against the person in England in the early to mid-1950s. It was a period in which offences like Stowe's were not uncommon. It would be possible to look for answers in the nature of the society at the time, and at the particular pressures such as rationing, poverty and the aftermath of the war. But in the end, here is a case in which there was motiveless malignity and a poor woman happened to be in the wrong place at the wrong time.

The answer for the culprit was a prison term.

The road by Laughton woods. The author

Laughton, a small village and woodland between Scunthorpe and Gainsborough, is a very quiet spot; the last thing anyone would expect to see there would be a violent crime, but it happened, and the statement made, however vacuous, was the only explanation offered at the time. The only news associated with the place in the twentieth century are the sightings of big cats in the forest.

Stowe, who lived at Ashby in Parker's Lane, was sent to trial for robbery with violence. He was not exactly careful and had made no attempt to conceal weapons: the hammer and some items belonging to Mrs Wraith were found in the hedges along the Laughton road. She picked Stowe out of an identity parade, and also easily identified the hammer he had used. Stowe was undoubtedly an inept and bungling criminal. He was married, and with a child, and the case then went to trial. He was a man with other offences in his past, such as larceny, but this was a step up on the scale of heinous crime.

He was far too dangerous to be allowed to walk the streets around Scunthorpe, and it is perhaps more worrying that the attack was done not in the streets but in a lonely stretch of road in North Lincolnshire where people were accustomed to being safe if they walked alone.

CHAPTER 30

Mother Kills Her Daughter
1953

... a sad case ... a stranger to herself.

In Doncaster, in September 1953, a woman walked up to a policeman brandishing a newspaper at him, saying, 'I am the woman you have been looking for. I murdered her.' The victim in question was her daughter, Lorna, and the killer was Mrs Eva Williamson, aged forty, who had been missing for over twenty-four hours since her husband had come to her home in Highcliff Gardens, Scunthorpe, and found the body of his young niece. This area is one of comfortable semi-detached homes, safe, peaceful and ordinary. The street would be the last place one would expect a brutal 'domestic' murder to take place.

This is a sad case. Remanded in custody and given legal aid, Eva was then taken to Manchester for specialist mental care. Something in her had snapped and an everyday domestic issue had led to her battering her daughter to death. Little Lorna, only fourteen, was a frail girl who went to Doncaster Road Girls' School. On the fateful day she had been at home from school on holiday. A mood and an altercation, normally settled after an emotional storm, led to something much worse.

The girl was found on the floor of the living room, bludgeoned to death, and the body discovered by her father Harry when he came home from work. He was a paint-sprayer at Appleby Frodingham and had come straight home after his shift. A telling detail is that the curtains were drawn to, suggesting that Eva had had some small twinge of emotion leading her to cover and enclose the awful thing she had done.

The hunt for her was soon in progress, as her absence suggested either guilt or perhaps abduction. There were some signs of a scuffle, and this led to police being concerned that she might have been taken and abandoned in one of the quieter areas close to the edge of town. They even brought in

The school Lorna attended on Doncaster Road. The author

dogs from as far away as Melton Mowbray. But then Doncaster CID phoned Scunthorpe to say the mother was in safe keeping, and Scunthorpe detectives went by car to collect her.

The disturbing sight of the mother in court the next day, very composed and simply dressed, calm and collected, must have been horrific for her husband, and indeed for her brother, Leonard Berridge, a salesman from Pontefract, who had the unenviable task of affirming the identification of the girl, as he saw her body on the evening of the killing – at around nine that Tuesday in fact. Eric Dyson held the first short hearing, at the hospital, and the identification was made there.

D S Knowler, who was in charge of the case, said that the mother would have special treatment and observation in Manchester. Dr Yager reported on the condition of the victim, saying that she was killed around one p.m. that Tuesday. The Home Office pathologist, Dr David Hamilton, joined Yager the next day and they concurred that the death was caused by multiple blows to the head and these caused several skull fractures. Eva was formally charged with the murder.

One major factor in the breakdown of the mother was that asthmatic Lorna had been a strain, being so needy and frail. Today, we might look to social support, to a whole range of professionals, and also there would be the factor of there being available communication outlets for a woman under stress. This is still no excuse for murder, and this was a savage version of that crime. In the end, the root cause was mental instability. Looking back at the story now, it is impossible not to feel immense sympathy for the relatives, and imagining the horror experienced by Harry Williamson at tea-time that September afternoon is almost beyond possibility.

The little woman he saw in the dock, with her tweed coat and fawn hat, must have seemed like a stranger to him. Tragically, she was also a stranger to herself.

CHAPTER 31

Arson at Midnight
1953
'I never thought it would flame up like this.'

Scunthorpe's *annus horribilis* went on relentlessly, this time with a home fire. The problem was that this was no blaze brought about by the careless flick of a cigarette-stub. This was deliberate.

This is a tale of a middle-aged man whose drinking habits led to the ruin of his life, and of his daughter, a heroine at the centre of the events, who prevented the outcome being even worse than it was. Frank Johnson was a labourer, living in Tomlinson Avenue in a council house. On an August night he had had one drink too many and when he came home, he was ready to cause a fight and to destroy anything in sight. He was so violent that his daughter Brenda barricaded herself and two

Tomlinson Avenue. The author

younger brothers into a room, wedging the door shut with a chair.

Brenda recalled that awful night for the benefit of the court, saying that her raving father had repeatedly shouted, 'I'll get seven years for this!' and that at one point he had stood at the bottom of the stairs wielding a chair and threatening to smash anyone who came near him. The trigger to a very desperate struggle between father and daughter came when, after he had ordered all the children to bed he raised an arm to his wife. This was too much for Brenda to tolerate; she grappled with him and they had a rough fight, Brenda biting his arm in response to him thumping her in the eye. She threw things at him as he raged and swore.

After being holed up in the room, Brenda heard Johnson yell that the house was on fire. He had made a trail of papers and comics all the way upstairs and a breeze had caused the curtains to blaze. Brenda dashed out, still showing plenty of zest for a confrontation with the drunken Johnson, and she put out some of the fire, which was not accelerating in effect. She said that she 'stamped on the carpets and fetched water to put on the flames around the window-frame and curtains.' Mrs Johnson ran to bring the fire brigade.

Brenda testified that her father had started a fire in her bedroom as well; she found a pile of blankets and matches there, and many had been burned and were smouldering. Burned matchsticks and papers were strewn everywhere. The fire officer who came and dealt with the blaze, Nathaniel Edmonds, said that when he arrived he found heaps of burned blankets, papers and clothing on the stairs. Some of these things had been completely destroyed.

When the police arrived, led by D S Ferriby, the husband and wife were now standing around, Johnson muttering about his seven-year sentence, and his wife pointing at him, stunned with disbelief, saying, 'He set the house on fire.' Ferriby confirmed that Johnson said he was responsible for the blaze. The statement Johnson eventually gave police while under arrest in Scunthorpe was that he had only meant to frighten the family. 'I wanted more or less to cause smoke … I was going to smother it out again but there seemed to be a draught which set the curtains on fire.'

DI Cottingham tried to prevent bail but it was nevertheless awarded. Prison did indeed await Johnson. The hapless, inept man with very little sense of reality could only say, 'This is through having a drink. I never thought it would flame up like this.'

It has to be brave Brenda Johnson who comes out of this as a most remarkable young woman; she took on the responsibility for the imminent distaster, and when she had no choice, she even engaged in what can only be called a 'dogfight' to overcome a man in a state of disregard and rage. The night had started with Brenda and her mother simply lying in bed, fearful of the man shouting downstairs, and had ended with a situation very close to total ruin of the home – and definitely the destruction of a marriage.

CHAPTER 32

A Street Stabbing
1953

Poor Jean felt a pain in her back, and fell to the ground.

Almost every week in the newspapers, various types of criminal events are called 'incidents' a word which starts to appear trivial by overuse. The columns of periodicals from the past often use the word, but by today's terms, a legal word can be used and suddenly an 'incident' changes from minor to serious. This was the case in the story of Kenneth Frow of Ashby and his attack on his wife.

Jean, Frow's twenty-two-year-old wife, was walking along Ashby High Street with a friend on a night in July, when she saw her husband approaching them. Frow paused for a moment and said something to his spouse; the friend could not make out what that was; then, in a matter of seconds, he stabbed her with some scissors and ran off. He had grabbed her by the lapels of her coat – a confrontational gesture, aggressive and eye-to-eye.

Poor Jean felt a pain in her back, and fell to the ground. She had to be taken to hospital, and it was found that she had two wounds, one severe, entailing stitches. The reason was a mystery, and the explanation was not sound enough to convince Frow's father and brother to stand and act for him in court. The man stood and had nothing to say except a pointless statement that 'My conscience is clear; I am innocent.' How anyone could say that when there was a witness to the attack is beyond belief. He had used the scissors only a few feet from where Jean's friend stood.

DI Knowler, who was having a busy summer as the violence continued, often in the streets and fuelled by drink, said that Frow had made two other statements asserting his innocence, and a more meaningful account of his state of mind at the time: that amounted to foundless jealousy, a mere suspicion of misconduct on his wife's part that had fed his anger. In court, only his mother acted for him. His father would say nothing at all. The detectives involved confirmed that it was a serious attack and pointed to the possibility of the man being dangerous to others, so they were not keen on bail being awarded. They insisted on two sureties, and they only had one. Frow's grandfather's name was put forward, but he also refused to act.

Then the terminology changed. The local paper had referred to an 'incident'; it began as malicious wounding, but further evidence and a re-think about the potential risk in the man's character, changed the charge to 'malicious wounding with intent to do bodily harm.'

The significance of this case is how representative it was of those years. In the years 1953–54 there was an average of three street crimes a day reported and one of these was a crime against the person; there were burglaries and petty thefts every day in the town. The most sensational crime of the year was a betting shop raid in which scores of men were arrested and four were eventually given custodial sentences. That was merely gambling – a licence problem. But all around the pubs and clubs there was too much drink and too much rage.

It would be hard to tell Mrs Frow that she lived in generous, sociable times when everyone pulled together in a communal spirit, particularly when her husband had a short spell behind bars.

CHAPTER 33

Terrible Neglect by a Brigg Couple 1953

... he found the child in a fully 'filthy and bedraggled state.'

t is a thousand pities that people like you should bring children into the world' – so said the NSPCC inspector when he reviewed the events around the shameful neglect of a baby by Kathleen and Francis Hales of Jameson Street, Brigg. Alderman Maxey, in charge of the hearing, agreed wholeheartedly. The couple had maltreated and neglected their two-year-old daughter, Elizabeth, on several occasions, and their lifestyle was indicative of a totally irresponsible attitude to the demands and responsibilities they should have had.

Their life story pinpoints the misery of that street-life that has always been with us in English history: they were virtually nomads despite their occasional life under a roof. The directive of the 1904 manual of the NSPCC, from the *Inspector's Directory*, makes it clear that such cases were not uncommon then, and even by the middle years of the century, after the social security and national health measures were in place, there were poor copers around who could be anything from 'feeble-minded' to 'dangerous to children in their custody.' The directory refers to 'the hopeless character of an offender' whose child must be taken into safe custody. There was no doubt about this in the Hales case.

The pair appear to have drifted across the area, from village to village, living aimlessly and with no work. Begging was their only activity, and that was not successful. Worse still, this was not their first offence in this regard: they had been convicted of the same act in 1950.

A witness reported that he found them in Louth looking worn and ill, and Mr Hales said that they had been 'sleeping rough' out at Hubbard's Hill. Another witness, a Mrs Melton, said that at one point she had taken them into her lodgings and had seen Mrs Hales hold the baby under a cold water tap to wash her. This was in Jubilee Crescent, Louth, at one of the rare periods in which the family had a roof over their heads.

The NSPCC inspector in the case said that when he had been called to them, he found the child in a 'filthy and bedraggled state'. He had found them huddled on a bench in Louth and their condition was 'despicably filthy'. He reported that the child had only some stale milk under a sheet in the pram. Mr Hales had no more than one penny on his person.

The amazing thing here is that even the young mother had no idea how to cope and had no knowledge of child care. Mrs Melton, when they were with her in the April, some months before they appeared in court, told the hearing that she had had to bath the child, but also she had to wash the mother as well. She described them on their arrival as 'verminous and filthy'. The family only stayed with her until June, and then had to leave, with no destination in mind. They ended up in Brigg again, and it is not clear how they managed to afford any lodgings at all; we can only guess at how they earned money when desperate – probably when they were actually starving.

A significant point here is that both had served a six-month prison sentence after the previous prosecution; their story illustrates the tendency of deprived and socially excluded people to accept that a gaol term is their only viable option when all else fails. They must have welcomed the bed, the food and the cleanliness of Lincoln prison. After all, they all needed care; there was something in their world-view that excluded the norms of self-respect and the willingness to accept the work ethic that was so important at that time. They were heading there again, to a place where their child would be clean and well fed. If it had not been for Mrs Melton, they may well have been destined for extreme suffering on the streets, in the open, with none of the basics of life.

CHAPTER 34

A Baffling Brigg Drowning
1954

Later questions seemed to show that there was a wall of silence.

The death of thirteen-year-old Brian Ladlow in Brigg, drowned in the river Ancholme, may have been purely accidental; but there may also have been suspicious elements to it. Whatever the truth is, the story presents us with a mystery. The Coroner, Mr Howden, asked police to make extensive enquiries about the incident, as there was no clear narrative of events available. Officers interviewed twenty-six witnesses yet still nothing conclusive was said or found.

The centre of this puzzling death is a strange contradiction. Iris Drayton, then thirteen and in the same class at school as Brian, led officers Hannath and Corney to the scene where she had seen Brian with his sister and then later she had seen Brian and Brian Neall playing with a large tube, saying they could have a game with it. All seemed clear-cut, but then Neall said he had never seen Brian that afternoon until a time very late in the day when he saw the boy in the middle of the river. The boy said he might have played about with one, but never went near anyone else. Brian had occasionally come out of the water to warm himself at a fire; he may well have been suffering from muscular problems at some point when he was swimming alone.

But of course questions had to be asked about any fooling around that might have led to rough play. A reporter at the time first broached the subject and referred to some statements insisting that no-one had been 'pushed off' one of the three tubes that were providing cheap entertainment for the children.

Someone was lying, or suffering from as much-impaired memory of events. Basically, the scene was summer, on a day when kids settled down from late morning through to the

The River Ancholme, Brigg. The author

evening at around seven, playing, talking and generally enjoying friendship. But Brian's brother, Barry, also told a story that was at odds with the others. The police must have been very confused.

Had some games gone wrong? Later questions seemed to show that there was a wall of silence. One of the crowd actually said that they did not know Brian at all, which seems very strange. The police enquiry was thorough and extensive; Mr Howden noted that Sergeant Gurney and his team had worked very hard: 'You have been to a tremendous amount of trouble and I appreciate it.' But most of the statements made threw no light on this tragic death at all. One of the officers said they had taken twenty-six statements but that the team could work 'from now until Christmas and it would not do any good.'

We are left with a death by misadventure. But somewhere under these facts there is the possibility of a terrifying accident, maybe something rash and spontaneous that led to the drowning. The truth will never come out, but through contemporary eyes, with accumulated wisdom of similar cases, the contradictions and denials point to a sub-plot to Brian Ladlow's death. The bare facts make one want to know much more, and to ask questions that were never reported, such as how good a swimmer was the boy? Did he have a history of risk-taking? Were there any factions in the group at play?

All this has sunk into oblivion, but one haunting statement hints at the untold story: Barry Neall's description of all the kids playing, swimming from one side to the other – and more importantly, that each tube belonged to particular people. The hint is that something like 'I'm the King of the Castle' got out of hand. But that's a guess, just a theory, and all deaths without a satisfying closure invite us to make our theories. The fact that very little direct evidence had been collected, when there were so very many witnesses, creates understandable suspicion in the mind of any objective investigator.

The secret is in and around the River Ancholme and in distant history.

CHAPTER 35

Two Attacks on Police Officers
1954

Douglas swore at the policeman, then hit him on the jaw and knocked him to the ground.

The mid-50s were not happy years for police officers. Street attacks were common, and in 1954 there were some normal drink and fight problems, but also some very odd cases.

PC Dennis Matthews's young son caused a lot of trouble one night in Ashby. He had been watching a programme called *Journey into Space* on television one night, and then decided to go wandering around the streets. His walk took him towards the home of William Douglas, in Wesley Road, and from then on, the boy seems to have spun a yarn, convincing Douglas that his father was in the habit of beating him.

When the constable, on his bike and searching for his son in the darkness of the late evening, finally came across Douglas, it was a heated exchange. The constable asked Douglas if he had seen a little boy, and the boilerman, who was now in Bellingham Road and clearly hunting for the man who had been so brutal to a small boy, said the child was in his home.

Douglas swore at the policeman, then hit him on the jaw and knocked him to the ground. Matthews had called for his son, after getting to his feet, and did not retaliate. Instead, he simply put the boy on the saddle and rode home. There was physical punishment in the Matthews household, but it came allegedly from the mother. But at the time, Douglas turned his venom on the man who had apparently abused a small boy. He threatened the officer, saying, 'If you touch the boy again I will murder you.'

Douglas's solicitor, H M Winocour, argued very convincingly that Douglas's moral indignation was the action of a thoughtful and caring civilised man, but the fact was that Matthews's jaw was broken, and Dr Robert Eminson stated that there were no marks on the boy to indicate harsh physical beatings. A A Collins, acting for Matthews, gave an explanation that matches the facts and events very well. He said that the boy had been ill, had nightmares, and had been suffering from a feverish condition for some days. It seems highly likely that his imagination had created a scenario to rival some of his comics' and television storylines. To make things worse, the boy was wearing pyjamas, giving the impression that he had run away from home in some haste and in a panic, at such an abnormal time to be out and about.

Emotions ran so high that Winocour actually reacted to Mrs Matthews's anger by saying that surely Douglas had saved her son's life? The woman was clearly in trouble, knowing that her husband had said that she would hit the child if any hitting had to be done. That did not help his case.

This tale has an element of black comedy, and is bizarre in the way it brings out communal attitudes at the time. But there is nothing amusing about the assaults on PC John Henderson and Sergeant Cuttell, who were attacked by a crowd of Irish labourers. Five of the attackers were destined for imprisonment, such was the ferocity of the violence unleashed that night.

It was a Wednesday night, and the labourers had been paid. There went on the usual pub crawl and turned nasty. The bunch seem to have been led by Desmond McCabe and Patrick Harte, two men in their twenties. The group had only been in the town for a few days, working for contractors on the steelworks. When officers had words with them outside the *Furnace Arms*, the response was unexpectedly savage. The two officers were thumped, kicked and struck with beer bottles as more men set about them. But two civilians had helped the police, one of them knocking McCabe to the ground. DI Cottingham in court made the point

Sergeant Cuttell. Laura Carter

that it was hard to distinguish who did exactly what in the affray, but one officer could only recall seeing heaps of broken glass before losing consciousness. Another officer, PC Henderson, limped into court. He said that McCabe broke a bottle on a nearby traffic sign and came at him with it. McCabe had also been seen kicking an officer as he was down on the road.

This kind of incident was not all that rare in the steeltown at that time. Contract labour touring the pubs and becoming unruly was common, and always likely to escalate into confrontations. But in 1954 there must have been a large number of police constables who thought they were not paid enough for the risks they ran – either near their homes or among the violent drunks.

CHAPTER 36

A Frenzied Killing on the Winterton Road
The Roberts Case 1955

He first strangled her with two hands, and then with her scarf.

The facts of this case are very straightforward on the surface: Kenneth Roberts, a man of twenty-four, married and living in Spencer Avenue, Scunthorpe, phoned police on the morning of 11 May 1955 to confess to a murder. He had strangled Mary Roberts (no relation) in a Winterton wood yard the night before, but that he did not kill her. His explanation was that he had 'gone crazy.' Roberts had used the girl's own chiffon scarf.

But the important detail was that he believed she was already dead when he applied the scarf to her neck. At his trial

The Winteron Road, showing British Oxygen Company: the area where Roberts struck. The author

in Nottingham he pleaded not guilty, but he was found guilty of murder and hanged at Lincoln prison on 12 July that year by Steve Wade, a man trained by the Pierrepoints. He had not made an appeal.

That is, of course, far too simple, and this was a major murder case. Mary Roberts, daughter of Violet of 25, Roxby Road, Winterton, enjoyed clubbing and drinking; she was not married, but had a child, and was expecting another that fateful night when she set off to Scunthorpe to enjoy a night out. When she left, very late that night, she met Roberts, who was on his bicycle at the time, and they started talking. Her lifestyle is naturally a relevant consideration here; being alone at that time of night is a chancy business.

The doctor on the scene at 2 am at the woodyard, said that she died around two hours earlier, consistent with the facts of her leaving the club. He had been called in the hope that she could be saved, but there was no possibility of that. Roberts had actually accompanied officers to the place of death, after making the call. Mary was having a tough time; her father, Wilfred, made the point that she had no job, although she had worked for a local wholesale newsagents for a time. A few months before she had been troubled with an attack of appendicitis. It is important to note that Dr Stanford, reporting on her condition after the autopsy, confirmed that this medical condition had no bearing on her death.

Inspector Tom Evinson confirmed that Roberts had made the call and led them to the woodyard. But his story remained the same, through to the trial at Nottingham: she had been dead before he acted. But he was remanded and charged with her murder and granted legal aid. Roberts, the warehouseman with two children, living a normal suburban life in a small provincial town, was to see his name in the national newspapers, but for all the wrong reasons. It was not to stay there long, because Ruth Ellis was hanged on 13 July.

The focus of the trial was on the strangling with the scarf. It was ascertained that he had picked Mary up with the intention of taking her to the woodyard for sex. It emerged that the girl started talking about other men she had known and something in Roberts snapped. He first strangled her with his hands, and then with her scarf. The problem was that the available medical evidence showed that it was the ligature caused by the scarf that killed her, not asphyxiation by hands. One line of thought for the defence was then clearly to assert Roberts' first claim that she had died by means of something Roberts *did not intend to use to kill her.* This tenuous claim was to bring in the possibility of a manslaughter charge. It did not work.

The Roberts story has the depressingly familiar theme of the cheap and seedy sexual adventures of the married man, and this linking with the type of young

Roberts' death recorded on HMP Lincoln gate. Laura Carter

woman who is out for 'a good time' and enjoys the liaisons of this kind, and the sense of risk and excitement they bring. But Roberts patently had other mental problems, personality traits involving rage and mood-swings always potentially triggered by situations of high emotion. Poor Mary Roberts had maybe had a few drinks and wanted some more fun of a different kind. She just happened to meet the wrong man at the wrong time.

Kenneth Roberts became the last Lincolnshire man to die on the county gallows: some small notoriety that puts him in the statistical records. From the moment he made the phone call, he was never going to have a chance of coming up with a plausible defence, and justice was done, as it was perceived at that time.

CHAPTER 37

A Neck-Tie Attack
Scunthorpe 1960

... Cox pulled the tie tighter and his victim passed out.

One of the quieter parts of the town is undoubtedly Brumby, and the streets around the area from the central park to Ashby are normally peaceful places with large gardens and determined home-makers. But the streets are also places where, in the black of night, predators of humans stalk and defensible space is hard to find. Within the last twenty years there have been two notable street attacks of extreme ferocity, including a murderous assault on an old man by two youths.

But forty-four years ago there was an attack on a young woman in Lloyds Avenue, a street usually thronging with students on their way to the former technical college today. But unemployed Barton man George Cox, a man with severe mental problems and sexual fixations, found the road to be a perfect place to brutally attack Jean Guesford.

He followed Jean as she walked home towards her house in Glover Road; as she became aware of some danger from him she broke into a run, but he caught her up and then threw a neck tie over her head. As she screamed in panic, Cox pulled the tie tighter and his victim passed out. But luckily, there was a witness, as someone living in Lloyd's Avenue saw all this happen, and ran to get help from the owner of the corner shop close to Glover Road. Both people then came to help the woman, but Cox ran away.

DI Darnell said that Jean was taken to hospital and was kept in for five days; fortunately, her wounds were not serious: bruises and cuts mainly, although her jaw was very badly bruised and she was in some considerable pain. The scars were mainly psychological, of course, after an ordeal like that. She had a lot to tell the police, though, eventually; but Cox

Ashby Road, where the attacker was seen earlier. The author

was even more loquacious, making statements to the effect that he was not involved, though he recalled the girl. He said, 'I cannot remember it. I cannot remember things very well. Without doubt, this was a pathetically unacceptable defence. When he added that there had been a meeting, with a girl who was taller than him with fair hair, he said he 'wanted to be friendly at first but she would not stop.' Then comes a statement from the attacker that tries to suggest a physical/mental problem, as he talked about a 'pain' he felt: 'Then I got my pain and I had to lay hands on her.'

The man was a dangerous psychopath; he described the pain in his stomach and then the urge to take out his tie and

Lloyd's Avenue, where the attack took place. The author

choke the woman. The usual account was given of taking out the tie 'to stop her screaming.' Things grew worse when he admitted a sexual assault on a young child in Scunthorpe market, and again, he related it to a pain that went over him and an urge to destroy.

Cox was clearly too much of a risk to be allowed on the streets and he was put away; As far back as 1952 he had committed an assault, and it transpired later that he was keen

Jean's home on Glover Road. The author

on child pornography and had a collection of such photographs in his possession when arrested. The final exchange after arrest was so banal that it says a great deal about this variety of psychopath. Cox said that he would 'not visit Scunthorpe no more' and Mr Haslam replied: 'It is not by attending Scunthorpe that you get into this trouble.'

CHAPTER 38

A Killing in the Steelworks
1966

... a bitter and savage fight, escalating to a point at which Yusef lost self control.

The various steel companies at Scunthorpe have always used immigrant labour and as the town has grown, the cultural diversity has been marked. Over the years, a wide spectrum of minority groups have been noticeable, some more thoroughly integrated than others. Today, there are many people from the Middle East in the area, and in the last thirty years there has been an influx of labour from these origins, often to work in specific parts of the works, such as the sinter plant in the 1970s. Naturally, different cultures bring with them different moral codes and ideologies. This murder case relates to this kind of experience, and was a very visible, remarkable attack in the course of a working day.

'The Three Queens' – blast furnaces where Salih worked. The author

Somali, Ahmed Yusef called out loudly, 'All of a sudden bad news spread all over the town because people said I was a pouf.' The man put the blame roundly on fellow steelworker from Aden, Mohamed Salih, and after a scuffle, knifed the man to death. There was some delay at court because Yusef had himself received some wounds and was receiving treatment on the day of the first hearing. It had been a bitter and savage fight, escalating to a point at which Yusef lost all self-control.

Salih had lived in Trafford Street in the town and Yusef in Gurnell Street; they knew each other well. Peter Abbot, for the Crown Prosecution Service, made the point that their fight was absolutely open and in front of others, a rare event in murder. He also said that at first there was no clear motive, and none could be found other than the killer's revulsion and sense of shame at being called homosexual. They both worked as furnacemen, Yusef on the Queen Anne furnace and Salih on the Queen Victoria.

A group of workers had become aware, early in the afternoon of 10 April, that there was a scuffle and some cursing. Heads turned and they saw the two men struggling and grappling with each other. Many noted the stabbing motion of one of Yusef's arms. Then, Yusef kicked his opponent down some stairs, rushed after him and set about the man with his knife. When bystanders eventually went to the wounded man, he was found to be bleeding from several knife-wounds and rushed to hospital – at the Scunthorpe War Memorial Hospital very close by, but he died soon after the attack.

It is amazing that such a prolonged and vicious attack continued without interference; obviously (and understandably) fellow-workers kept out of the way of the flashing blade, as the assailant was in a wild frenzy. Such a confrontation may well have been one way that grudges were settled in these men's own culture, but the spectacle of such a fight was alarming in the middle of a shift in an English industrial plant.

The knife wound that did the most damage was alarmingly deep; Salih's back had been penetrated by a four-inch depth of blade, in at the back and through to the chest. When the killer

Gurnell Street. The author

was faced with the reality of what he had done, all he could say was, 'I kill him … I kill him.' The real beginning of the flare-up had come when Salih had said to Yusef, 'You are a pouf and a woman.' Then he slapped Yusef's face and the man's reaction was immediately to knife him. One can only relate this to a medieval challenge; some code of honour was at play here, and the response was quick and serious. With hindsight, it is difficult to see why Salih made such a public and insulting remark when he would have known the likely consequences. But both were in the grip of irrational, highly emotional states of mind and threw caution to the wind.

Yusef himself, according to an examination conducted by Dr R Foxton, had no wounds, and had only a scratch on his face. It is not difficult to see that this man was subject to terrible rages, and that his sense of honour and reputation was more central to his self-concept than anything else: the ultimate insult led to the ultimate crime and he went to gaol.

CHAPTER 39

Armed Raider at Bigby Road Post Office 1966

When the old lady turned away, the girl pulled a gun ...

Some crimes are one-off mysteries. A villain does something rash or dramatic and the local impact is quite profound, the shock often intense. But then there is no follow-up and the story fades away. Maybe the perpetrator never struck again, or moved to some area far away. This seems to be the case with the attack on this quiet post office in May 1966. At heart, this is a case of heroism, or downright foolhardiness.

Even more remarkable in this story is the fact that the armed bandit was a girl. She held up the postmistress with a gun; the

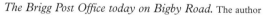

The Brigg Post Office today on Bigby Road. The author

robber simply marched into the shop and pointed a gun at Mrs Annie Watson, who was sixty-three years old. Mrs Watson normally had time to do some ironing when it was quiet, but nothing could have prepared her for this. Yet, the woman grappled with the armed robber and managed to disarm her.

The girl ran off, jumped on a green motor scooter and drove away in an easterly direction. It was late in the afternoon. Police were quick to act and set up roadblocks. It seemed that the young attacker had vanished. It was a small, quiet part of Brigg and even now is on a quiet side street off the centre. But forty years ago this was indeed a tranquil spot – the last place on earth you would expect an armed robbery, and is best described as a quiet side road, close to the main road to Bigby.

Mrs Watson was interviewed and said that she had heard a knock at the door and went through to the shop (from her ironing) and saw 'a girl of about twenty wearing a white crash-helmet.' It cannot have been much of a helmet as her face was clearly visible. The girl had some sort of plan, though, because she gave the postmistress a shilling and asked for some stamps. When the old lady turned away, the girl pulled a gun and when Mrs Watson turned around it was pointing right at her. Amazingly, Mrs Watson's reaction was to shout 'You little devil!' and then to take hold of her wrist and fight with her for possession of the gun. The intrepid woman, even after giving chase, called down a car driven by local farmer, Edward Chatterton, but he could not quickly get into to Caistor Road. He was quick-thinking enough to immediately dial 999.

The girl had been seen just a few minutes before the raid, and nothing was stolen. She even left her shilling behind. Again, police were sharp, and soon had information that the girl had been seen in a shop in Snitterby, a few miles down on the A15 to Lincoln, buying matches. That has the hallmark of the nervous, tentative criminal trying out the plan, moving closer to actual crime, and a crime involving a gun takes a considerable amount of resolve and determination. Mrs Watson was praised by police, and she even handed over the gun – which turned out to be an air pistol, to the law. Whether her daughter, Maureen, was so quick to praise her mother, is not certain.

This was the year in which several sub-post offices across the country had been robbed, and by people at gun-point. The officials and union representatives at national level were stating their concern, particularly after the murder of a postmistress in central Leeds in that same year. The rural Lincolnshire offices were put on special alert, and nothing was repeated. It looks as though Mrs Watson put an end to an incipient Bonnie without Clyde villain.

More than likely, the girl was full of the adrenalin rush of such a crime and moved on elsewhere to repeat the crime.

CHAPTER 40

The Unsolved Stephenson Case
1969

... fifteen thousand people were interviewed.

At his large and lonely house on the Barton-Barrow road in April 1969, Robert Stephenson lay for several days, gagged and wounded, after a horrendous ordeal at the hands of two robbers who struck him with iron bars, and then left him to die. The seventy-year-old had been shut up in one room with no food or water, and the house had been ransacked. He lasted long enough in hospital to say that he thought his attackers spoke with Irish accents. They took only £8 and walked out into obscurity; despite a few leads in the time shortly after the murder, the case remains unsolved.

Stephenson was a recluse who collected antiques and owned fifty-one acres of land in the area, as well as some property in Hull. He had a great deal of property, and one of the main problems for the police at the time, as DCI Bob Kirk told the papers in 1994 when he recollected the case, was that no-one knew exactly what had been in there. The rumours were that there were gold sovereigns and Dresden china. Certainly, much was left there, and auctioned later at Brigg Corn Exchange. On 18 October 1970 the hoard fetched around £1,000. Much of this had been coins, silver and jewellery.

The case was re-opened in 1989 after a 'tip-off' in the form of an anonymous telephone call. By that time, the affair had been generally known as the 'Hermit Murder'. The basic facts of the torture of his ordeal, the theft and the finding of the poor man by his neighbour, John Rigg were known. The old man had been woken at midnight and been battered on the head by iron bars. New enquiries were made, and fresh searches, in the light of the call, but to no effect. Rigg bought his neighbour's home in 1971.

At the time, the enquiry escalated into many areas of the land; by 26 April, another group of twenty detectives were drafted into Barton, making a total of one hundred and twenty men on the case. DCI Joseph Camamile of Lincolnshire CID led the chase, and he had some details of two Irishmen they were looking for. But leads and connections led as far away as Berkshire and also to Harlsden, North London. But the main lead was the 'Irish' reference of the dying man, and sure enough, after identikits and other statements, there was a determined search locally for a 'rough-looking Irishman' who had called at a house four miles from Barton. He had been

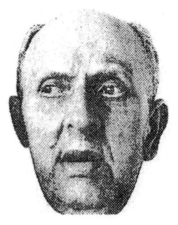

Mr Stephenson: battered during the night. Scunthorpe Evening Telegraph

seen near Bonby Lodge after calling at Horkstow House to ask for food and drink.

A torch-light search was started across Saxby Wolds, and fifteen thousand people were interviewed. The Irishman was seen running towards Horkstow Top. Check-points were set

The isolated house where Mr Stephenson was held for seven days without food or water

up and police were issued with flares. Camamile admitted he had no definite connection, but noted that there must have been some reason for the man in question to run off.

The headquarters of the Barton manhunt was the focus of a large-scale operation. As the local paper pointed out, 'The top men from the CID' were there, including the Deputy Chief Constable, Albert Brown, who knew the area very well indeed. Thirty-nine men travelled from Grimsby and Scunthorpe every day, so the small town on the Humber had to adapt sharply and provide for them. The scale was enormous, but led to no arrest.

In the end we have a story of a killing of a lonely but wealthy man in an isolated area by two desperate men who were never caught. For several weeks, gangs of police officers covered the Barrow, New Holland and Barton areas, but eventually to no avail. The story is, nevertheless, one of the central character – the victim. Stephenson was formerly a collector of second-hand clothes for a small business, and then his father left him money and property. He was worth £10,000 but had never signed a will; he was thought of as a timid, harmless eccentric who lived with his cat, Johnny. He was born in Barrow, but his family had had business interests in Hull for some considerable time. His elderly neighbours said that sometimes, they would not see him around for a period of several months, as he was essentially a recluse. He was an intelligent man, always smartly dressed, they said. His passion was to buy things that no-one else seemed to want, and to hoard them.

The reporters at the time made much of Johnny; they made him the 'only witness' to

Police issue pictures

LINCOLNSHIRE police today issued identikit pictures of two men they wish to question in connection with the murder of 69-years-old Mr. Robert Stephenson, at Barton-on-Humber.

The men were seen in the Barton area between April 9 - 13.

Man No. 1: 30 - 35 years, 5ft. 9in., stocky built, thick

bushy ginger hair, combed forward over forehead; pock-marked complexion; believed wearing khaki battle-dress blouse under a fawn overcoat.

Man No. 2: 35 - 40 years, height 5ft. 10in. to 6ft.,

medium build, dark hair brushed back, believed wearing a dirty fawn raincoat.

Identikits issued at the time. Scunthorpe Evening Telegraph

the terrible attack. He eventually went to a Scunthorpe cattery where he was well cared for. The cat was a local star for some time during the enquiry.

We have, then, an unsolved case, and time goes on. Sergeant Blackell, at the inquest, had said, ''I don't know if they were Chinamen or Irish. They had iron bars.' The officer then said that the dying man had said it had been a long time since he had been to see him. The heart of this case is that powerful mix of the inscrutability of the hermit and the puzzle of his brutal murder. The officer's laconic statement sums up much of the nature of this nasty and inhuman killing in the countryside.

It was a very high profile affair: the media reporting of the murder and the most complex aftermath, was indicative of the vicarious pleasures of such macabre crimes at that time. Television was exploiting violent British crime narratives at

The incident room, Barton. Scunthorpe Evening Telegraph

The incident room, set up at Barton-on-Humber Police Station. Police officers examine every detail of information brought in by inquiries. In the picture are : Det.-sgt. I. Jefferson (Grimsby), Det.-sgt. R. Chandler (Scunthorpe), Det.-sgt. R. Dickinson (H.Q.), and Det.-con. P. Greaves (Gainsborough).

this time, and killings such as this were given a new kind of attention, often bordering on the unhealthy vicarious pleasures of the 'schlock' magazines. The need to report ridiculous details such as the man's wealth, the cat going missing, and the apparently happily busy and excited local officers chatting in a café in Barton: it all has the ring of a new drive to indulge in the paraphernalia of a murder search, and Mr Stephenson's friends must have found it hard to take.

CHAPTER 41

Father Attacks Son
1971

... nothing was going to stop him behaving like a man possessed.

Hibaldstow has been in the news in very recent times, and for a suspicious death, when a sky-diver fell to his death in 2003. The tiny village on the roadside only a few miles off the main road south to Lincoln, is not more than a scattering of houses. Even today, the rural culture is evident: there are stables only a hundred yards from a new housing estate. But the place, with its very old Saxon name (Hubald's place) has seen other crimes.

In the early years of the twentieth century, the village had a lock-up, a place on East Street which is now a house next to the Methodist Chapel. So the area had seen some fights and confrontations centred on labourers who had taken too much ale. But this is a crime that came from something much more deep in the heart of a father with a simmering sense of outrage and disgust.

The Wheatsheaf, *Hibaldstow.* The author

In July 1971, Norman Shadlock appeared at the Lindsey Quarter Sessions on a charge of assault and the use of a firearm in a dangerous manner. He lived at West End, a very peaceful place, no more than a country lane, by old dairymen's cottages. It is a place with a long manorial history and enjoys a placid pace of life – most of the time, at least. The object of the man's wrath, and indeed the person at the wrong end of the barrel, was his own son.

He may not really have intended to endanger life, but he came very close to doing so.

The problem was that his son, in Norman's opinion, had an aversion to work. There must have been a long history of nagging, pressure and some forceful language behind this family story, because something snapped that July when Norman came home after having a drink or two. First he set about the lad with his fists, and it must have been a vicious attack; the young man protected himself from the blows raining down on him, and eventually retreated to the bedroom. His father was now screaming that he meant to shoot his son and went to find his gun.

The son's account was that suddenly, after a lull, he became aware of a gun-barrel at the window. Norman's voice yelled, 'Put your head through the window and I'll bloody shoot you.' His son, Graham, went to hide behind a door. It must have seemed that the man had snapped and may well have been serious. Then pellets cracked against the wall by the window.

When Shadlock was questioned, he said, 'I only did it to frighten him!' It later emerged that he had been brooding about his son's reluctance to do a day's work for some time, and said, in court, 'Why should I work seven days a week to keep him?'

This was a situation that had come along after too many silences and refusals to talk it through. The moment came when it was all too much, and this usually mild and quiet man let all the rage out. It might be called a 'mid-life crisis' as he was fifty-one, and subject to those aspects of extreme mood swings that go along with that stage of life; it may have been overwork, which is totally ironical when the reasons for the attack become clear. Whatever the reason, on that evening nothing was going to stop him behaving like a man possessed.

The landlord of *The Wheatsheaf*, a former police constable named Geoffrey Guest, said that Shadlock was an ideal customer: 'I've never known him be violent or lose his temper. This was entirely out of character for the man.'

All along, Shadlock had denied that he intended to do any harm and endanger life, but that was the main charge. Needless to say, his gun was taken away and kept by the police. He was lucky to be given probation. But the luck in truth was the fact that he had not killed his own son: that could easily have happened. It was confirmed at the trial that he had committed actual bodily harm. Certainly he had beaten his son, but wounds were limited by the lad's robust and desperate defence of himself. The regulars at *The Wheatsheaf* knew all about it, as they were subject to a dramatic performance that was very much out of the ordinary.

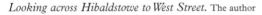

Looking across Hibaldstowe to West Street. The author

CHAPTER 42

The Killer Constable
1971

The images of the time show a cluster of busy and concerned senior officers around the ordinary semi-detached house, and a sense of high drama.

On 30 June 1971, PC Graham Wood was remanded in custody for the murder of his wife, Glenis. Her body had been found in the early hours of the morning at their home in Riddings, Scunthorpe, at 28, Kirkby Road. D S Miller Patrick was in charge, and Inspector R A Smith was first on the scene. A mobile police station was set up, and Dr Alan Usher, from Sheffield, came to carry out the post-mortem. This, as everyone then realised, was going to be a tragic case: one that led to a sentence passed of life imprisonment for the twenty-three-year-old.

Wood lived in an area with several other police houses nearby. Riddings is a large suburban area of the town with a large population confined in a labyrinth of streets. But as a more general policy, the town had adopted the idea of police houses in the area, as that neighbourhood was also bordering on Westcliff, a place which has had some problems with crime in recent decades.

The killer had a two-year-old daughter and there was another child on the way. But Wood was having an affair, and with a woman police constable (a person who had nothing at all to do with the crime, and this was confirmed at the trial). On the night of 28 June he had requested that he could be put on a different beat, saying that he had some investigations to close in particular areas. But it turned out that he wanted to be around near his own home at that time. Then, very early on the next day, central control lost all contact with Wood. It also transpired that Wood had been working hard to make it seem as though his wife had been killed by someone who wanted revenge on the officer, and when arriving home with his colleague after doing the murder, he tried to show that he thought there had been a break-in.

There was a long-standing story he told colleagues, concerning his receiving threatening letters, and as he had a lift back home on the morning on which his wife's body was to be found, and as he asked his friend in for a drink, Wood went into the bedroom and found his wife lying dead, strangled by the flex of an electric kettle. There was a letter beneath her body – one that turned out to be a 'threatening letter'. It was clearly an effort to put on a performance to match the seemingly meticulous preparation of the murder scene with the rather patently artificial details and 'clues'. It did not take long before he fell apart and confessed.

28, Kirkby Road. The author

On 28 June, the murder enquiry started in earnest. Dr Alan Usher, the Home Office pathologist, conducted a post-mortem on Mrs Wood. The reports at the time noted that a commando squad was brought in, and other staff from Lincoln and Grimsby, as a search began. It did not take long for a search to be undertaken, and dogs were used in this also. The images of the time show a cluster of busy and concerned senior officers around the ordinary semi-detached house, and a sense of high drama.

At the hearing, held the day after, the coroner, Mr Alan Collins, adjourned the inquest. But some of the facts of the case came out at that time, such as that Sergeant John Cooper, the brother of the victim, identified Glenis, and it was at this point that her pregnancy was confirmed.

As the process went on, there were several adjournments and extensions of remand, but Wood finally went to trial at Leicester in November. The full events of the night of the killing then emerged. He had been having a relationship with a woman colleague, and they had talked about his obtaining a divorce from Glenis. On this night, he had been working the night shift in Ashby, to the south of Scunthorpe centre, and this had clearly been done so that he was near to where the 'other woman' in the case lived. He had left her a note stuck on his car after spending some time in the police club. They met later on, she driving to Ashby to collect him; he was then not seen by any other officer on the beat and he did not answer calls, later insisting that his radio had been faulty. Finally, he was found and collected to have some refreshments, by Messingham Road (close to Ashby High Street). When he took a lift home from PC Rogers, the latter noted that, on arrival, he had seen that some of the doors were open after he had been invited in for some tea, and he had asked about Mrs Wood, and whether she would like a drink. Shortly after this she was found, half out of bed, and after a doctor was called to attend, her death was certified and it was clear that she had been strangled. Wood had killed her as she slept.

After a long period of adjournments, the trial lasted only ten minutes and Wood pleaded guilty. Mr Justice Bristow had little to do that day but to listen and then pass sentence.

As with all small towns, there are stories in the quiet suburbs that shock the local people: this was a notable example of this type of crime. In the long stretch of suburbs from the central part of the town out to Riddings, the streets have known their share of killings: knifings in the peaceful crescents and wife-murder in the front rooms. But there was something especially alarming in the fact of a police officer committing such a terrible crime in a 'police house' and the aftermath is still there in the memories of older residents.

The conclusion of this tragic story has to be that, whatever the emotional entanglements and personal relationships that would be central to the story, the end is that a twenty-three-year-old man was given a life sentence: a man who had clearly given the world the semblance of being a happy family man. Charles McCullough's defence at the trial, put this succinctly and powerfully: he said that if he had not done this terrible thing, 'he would now have a wife whom he loved, a daughter of two and a son aged six weeks. And he would still have been a police constable.'

It has been noted that the day after the murder, Wood wrote a letter to his colleagues in the force. That must have been a very hard thing to do.

CHAPTER 43

Double Murder in Grosvenor Street
1971

... a truly frenzied attack ...

Tragedy certainly hit the Sarneckyz family in Scunthorpe in 1971. First, Maria's son, Stephen, was killed at the steelworks, where he was working on a blast furnace. Then, just a few weeks later, her husband, Iwan was found dead, together with Mrs Margaret Dembizky, at her home in Grosvenor Street.

The various immigrant communities in the town had always maintained their cultural habits and sense of community, but at the time it seemed to many (wrongly of course) that the East Europeans had the habit of some kind of blood-feud. Such was the ridiculous media panic at the time. Certainly, some memories of the event from older residents convey a sense of outrage akin to the cinematic representation of the Mafia. 'That's the way they do things there' was a phrase one respondent told me, as if your Saxon English were somehow not capable of extreme crime.

Detective Inspector Felgate told the coroner at the inquest that both had been found stabbed to death. It had been a truly frenzied attack: the Ukrainian Sarneckyz had suffered multiple wounds to several parts of his body; Mary had been mostly attacked on the chest. The Sarneckyz couple had been divorced a year previously. Poor Maria had to come and identify her husband's body. Her husband had been found in the street, but Margaret Dembizky was found in a 'ten-foot' nearby at Burke Street. She had managed to struggle to her feet and walk a short distance.

Felgate made it clear that the police had the killer: Mr Metro Dembizky, a man known generally as Frank. Frank was also injured and admitted to hospital, but was not seriously injured. There had indeed been a major fracas, and Frank had earlier barricaded himself in the house. Police with tracker dogs surrounded the property. The killer had simply sat at the top of the staircase, a knife in each hand, and taken on the might of the police force. It is a notable feature of the red-brick houses of Crosby that there is a network of alleys running through them from the town centre to the Normanby end of town. Margaret was found in one of these: a dark place, out of public view.

The story had yet more complications, as there were three children in the house, and although these had not been harmed, there was clearly a dramatic sense of risk and vulnerability there. Eventually detectives convinced Frank that his best move was to let the children out, and he did so. The main negotiator was Chief Constable George Terry. His feat on that awful day must be prominent in his memoirs, as he was the hero of the hour. He must have provided onlookers with high drama as he talked to Frank Dembizky for a quarter of an hour, and as he did this, two officers entered the house

Part of Grosvenor Street. The author

by using a ladder. The man had clearly cracked and was emotionally unsound. But he was now wounded and taken to hospital to await the inquest.

Yet the real story behind this monstrous killing was never known: on the 18 September, a day before the court appearance, reported now by his proper name of Dymitre (not Frank, nor Metro) he hanged himself. He was found swinging in a hospital room in Lincoln prison. So he never walked into the Scunthorpe courtroom, and the clearly complex and profoundly disturbing details of the case were never aired in public.

The Burke Street Ten-Foot. The author

On the same day that the killings were first reported, a woman locally had died as a result of a wasp-sting. That is highly unusual, and the story made the front page, but the bloody confrontation in that Scunthorpe street made not only the local headlines, but the national papers too. Under that short period of heated and manic attack, there surely lies a narrative of passion, hatred and perhaps even a kind of possessive love. The one sure fact is that, although the town at the time had its share of street crime, it was not prepared for anything of this stature, in which two lives were lost, and people were bleeding to death in the open air.

CHAPTER 44

The Mystery of Christine
1973

The search for her was intense and determined ...

In May 1973 there was very inclement weather in the Scunthorpe area. It was cold and wintry. Around the streets where the Markhams lived in Robinson Road, there were extensive roadworks in progress, the Council were doing sewerage work and excavation. It was not a pleasant day for a search, and when the search was for a young girl who had not been seen in school, it was even worse.

Young Christine Markham had been to Ashby on the day she disappeared. She had gone to see a relative but never come home. Christine was seen at times, such as one sighting on Frodingham Road, and by another person at around midnight, but that may not definitely have been her. All kinds of possibilities arose when it came to a search for her. The part of Crosby where she lived is close to Ferry Road and to the area of natural beauty called Atkinson's Warren (Akkie's Warren locally) and the detectives in charge made sure that this area was thoroughly searched; police divers were also involved.

The police drew a circle on the map and went to every dwelling. Only one occupier refused them entry, and that was not a wise move. The man in charge was the charismatic Scot, Miller Patrick, who had been previously in the Grimsby Borough and came into the force at a time when a number of professional footballers were recruited, and he had plenty of ideas. But all kinds of false leads and dead-ends came along, even the appearance of a diary, found behind a bar in a pub, which turned out to be a red herring. Steadily, the search widened to include rubbish tips and rivers, back yards and cemeteries. Obviously, paedophiles were checked out and offenders in certain prisons were visited.

As time went on, some questions about criminals in a wider context had to be asked. In that respect, two lines of enquiry began: one concerned a man called Joe Kappen, who had lodged in the Scunthorpe vicinity in that year, and he had earlier been a suspect in some murders that took place in South Wales (the cases of Pauline Floyd, Geraldine Hughes and Sandra Newton); Christine had disappeared on May 21 and was never seen again. Kappen is known to have lived in Gainsborough, only fourteen miles way, at the time, and he worked in Scunthorpe as a lorry driver.

Christine Markham. Laura Carter

But as I write in 2004, police are opening up enquiries with the use of DNA. Kappen died of cancer in 1990. The only really significant statement in relation to Kappen (but no link being made to Christine) is that the Welsh police are not looking for anyone else in connection with the three killings in their domain. D S Philips has recently stated that, had Kappen been alive, he would 'more than likely have been charged' with the Welsh murders.

Frogmen searched for Christine. Laura Carter

Atkinson's Warren. The author

More notoriously, there is also the possibility that the serial killer, Robert Black, paid a visit to Scunthorpe. We know that he was responsible for three deaths; he was convicted for the murders of Lawrence, Aram and Fabb; the latter case, that of young April Fabb being taken while on her bicycle in Norfolk in 1969, led to the pinpointing of some parallels to the Scunthorpe disappearance, and this was followed up. But to say with any certainty (as some writers on web sites have said) that Black abducted Christine is something that cannot be condoned.

A meeting in 1994 in Newcastle was held to look at the possibility that Black was implicated in several murders other than the definite ones, and these even included cases abroad in Europe. But the Markham case was on the list. All that can really be said is that his modus operandi could fit the circumstances, but that is only a very vague line of thought. He is serving ten life sentences for the murder of the three girls.

Is the truth quite simply that the girl fell into some road-workings and, in the cold weather, died of cold or even hurt herself severely so that she could not move out from her temporary hiding-place? There has to be a possibility that this happened, and if she came somewhere near home and saw a line of police-cars by her gate she may have panicked and run to some place which eventually became the last place she occupied. The search for her was intense and determined, but a time comes when the costs of the operation are too high and other priorities come along. After all, 5,000 gardens and out-houses had been turned over, just to be sure that she was not there, close by, after all. A team of one sergeant and four constables set about combing the nearby streets – even at one point searching a false roof. So everything that could be done was done at that time.

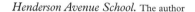

Henderson Avenue School. The author

CHAPTER 45

Masked Raid by Dangerous Men
1974

... one of the most callous of the crimes assembled in the research for this book.

I n the Scunthorpe area, the year 1974 was a time when several features of local crime could be pointed out, and a turning point brought about. One feature was the increase in drug-related robbery, and another was that there was a staff re-shuffle in the local police force. A survey of the newspapers at the time suggests a year of a great number of violent offences. One of the worst was to take place in the heart of the town. It would not be too much of an exaggeration to call this attack part of a reign of terror by a group of men.

The Recorder at Grimsby Crown Court in February of that year had a tale to tell about a merciless and brutal attack on an old lady in her own home. Two men broke into the home of Mrs Jones in Sheffield Street, Scunthorpe, wearing black stockings over their faces, and left her with, as the Recorder said, 'A memory that would remain with her for the rest of her life'.

When the seventy-year-old tried to bang on the wall for help, one of the assailants tried to choke her. It was indeed one of the most callous of the crimes assembled in the research for this book. One of the men, Richard Lefley, was jailed for four years, and his younger companion, Nigel Finch, was given a twenty-one month sentence. He was only seventeen, and Vernon was twenty-one.

They were no less than a couple of urban bandits, with a trail of theft and mayhem behind them. Young Finch asked for no less than eight other offences to be taken into account when he spoke at the trial. They had robbed Mrs Jones of money and a silver case: hardly a catch worth any kind of violence, to say nothing of the ordeal they put the old lady

Formerly the Lord Roberts Hotel, *a favourite place for these hard men.* The author

through. The case shocked the town in that year. Lefley was a hard case with a long record of burglary across the area; he had broken into a Doncaster Road café and also robbed a home in Crowle.

As the story unfolded it became clear that there was a large gang involved here: other secondary villains were also in court. There was a network of thefts, fences and outlets in the case, and the men involved were all young and reckless. Raymond McLaughlin, only eighteen, was in the burglary caper and had taken over £200 worth of cash and goods: he went to prison also. John Revell, of the same age, was involved in both burglaries and was sent to Borstal. The train of crooks went down even to a sixteen-year-old who received stolen goods and was given a supervision order.

What actually happened on that day when petty theft and burglary went to another level of violence was that, according to Mark Cursham for the prosecution, the preparatory moves had been made by Finch ingratiating himself into the Jones family and becoming friendly with the victim's grand-daughter. But nevertheless, they were still disguised when they broke in, and they ran upstairs to where the old lady slept, to demand money. Lefley took hold of her and handled her very roughly. The intimidation was extreme, and the woman began to scream in fear; at this point, the thug said he would strangle her. She feared for her life, of course, and at the time felt that her heart would suffer an attack through the stress and terror.

Even when Mrs Jones was allowed to go downstairs for a drink of water, she found another hooded figure: this was Finch. If the gang had planned to put her through mental torture of some length and intensity, they could not have planned it better. At that point, she was shoved down into a chair and told that she could be knifed if she was not attentive to their demands. During this part of the ordeal, under threat, and expecting a knife to be produced, Mrs Jones tried to bang on the wall. She would indeed have been heard. The houses in Crosby, all in the network of red-brick terraces, had thin walls in those days. But Lefley would have none of that and he grabbed her at her neck and began choking her. Cursham

Another area close by which they targeted. The author

made the point that this was vicious and intense: 'He pressed his thumbs into her throat so hard that she could hardly breathe.'

The final phase of the attack was a ransack of her bedroom by the whole gang, while she sat petrified with fear, expecting to be murdered, as she later said. The only defence offered was that they were told that there was a good haul to be had at the

Spencer Road, site of a similar crime a little earlier. The author

house, but that they were shocked to find Mrs Jones there when they entered. The words he spoke in court were unbelievably feeble as he said that he was sorry and that he, Lefley, had 'no intention of hurting her.' No-one that day was convinced of the truth of any of that. Finch claimed that he wanted to be out and have no part of the affair when the violence occurred. The younger ones had the usual excuses of being involved only on the margin, and that they were suffering from a 'compulsion' and so needed help.

But the core of this terrible attack is that, even if the thugs were not expecting anyone to be in the house, they behaved in such a way that suggested their determination to grab anything of value that they could, exploiting the situation to instil terror and abject misery into the poor seventy-year-old victim.

CHAPTER 46

The Unsolved Park Murder
Ashby, 1978

It was a terrible sight for the three steelworkers who found the body in that state.

On 22 December, 1978, Walter Taylor, only seventeen-years- old, had been to a dance at the Frodingham Community Centre. He walked towards his home in Ashby about a mile away, walking directly up Ashby Road, the main route south from Scunthorpe centre. Instead of going all the way to the T-junction at the end of the road, he cut through Jubilee Park. This is a small park alongside the St Bede's School, at that time popular for Sunday football and with a children's play area. Walter never reached his home in Victoria Road, Ashby. He was found early the next morning, battered to death.

He was lying on his back, and there was tissue paper around his neck; a piece of Scots pine was found close by, and it was stained with blood. Nevertheless, there is no definite proof that this was the weapon used. He had died from head wounds, however, and the pathologist had noted that the wounds could have been caused by repeated kicking. It was a terrible sight for the three steelworkers who found the body in that state.

The enquiries centred on Walter's movements and on a number of sightings which made tracing his movements in the hours before his death very difficult. For instance, he had been seen in Rowland Road (not far from the place where the dance was held); then, someone who could have been him was seen being

Walter Taylor. Laura Carter

sick further along towards Ashby at Revesby Avenue. This would be consistent with his taking the short-cut, as that road leads directly to the snicket through to the park. But if this was him, then two hours had passed between the two main sightings. He had apparently travelled only around a quarter of a mile in those two hours.

As the hunt for the killer or killers began in earnest, a complex picture of the movements of various gatherings of people on that night was put together, and there were in total thirteen groups or pairs of people seen around the streets in the area around Jubilee Park at that time. Logically, the closest position for any suspects to have been seen was close to Ashby High Street, but such sightings as two youths seen climbing over the park gates and four people seen walking into Belmont Street around midnight were never conclusively found and sorted. Certainly, Belmont Street was very close to the scene of death.

Walter was a sociable type, and when he did not return the next morning, it seemed natural to assume that he had stayed over with a friend. But his mother was to find out what had happened in a very dramatic and shocking way; she was in Mill Road Club and heard someone say that there had been a murder and that a young lad wearing black clothes had been found dead. Mrs Taylor said, 'That's our Walter!' She was sure of this after hearing the description. So began her campaign to find out how he died. She is on record as having worked constantly to increase the efforts, even to the extent of asking that Scotland Yard be brought into the case investigations.

The local force did indeed work hard also; CS John Crawley was involved and he set up a mobile police station in a nearby street. DS Ron Smith organised the search. The Home Office pathologist from Sheffield, Dr Alan Usher, was present also. A massive trawl began, across a wide area, officers working house-to-house. Over eight thousand people were interviewed, and then a reward was offered. There was no outcome. The search spread further than the Scunthorpe area and seventy potential suspects were cleared. Other detectives took over later, and the focus was obviously on looking for a motive. Writers have already expressed the range of potential motives, but these all depend on situations yet to be established firmly, such as the possibility that Walter was making enemies in some way. Words such as 'revenge attack' have been in print; the only sure thing is that robbery was not a motive as there was no evidence of any attempt to steal from him.

On the twenty-fifth anniversary of the murder, a report was published focusing on D I Tony Garton, with a picture of him

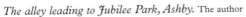
The alley leading to Jubilee Park, Ashby. The author

looking through the voluminous police files on the case. The feature noted two interesting details: first that the body was found near the centre of the football pitch, and second that the men seen clambering over a fence on Lindley Street who were never traced, may well hold the key to the case. We have a description: both were short, in their early twenties, wearing jeans, and eating from cardboard cartons. As to the scene on the football pitch – was this meant to convey something of significance about the killers and some kind of intended irony linked to their victim's life?

It was not until 1986 that an inquest recorded a verdict of unlawful killing. The hope now is that more advanced DNA techniques will bring something out of the file materials and people involved all those years ago. The case remains as the longest unsolved murder in the recent Humberside Police annals. Local people recall the case clearly, and talk still periodically turns to the death of that young man whose smiling face and long hair remain the abiding image of him, as

The football pitch where the body was found was here: now a playground. The author

in the *Evening Telegraph* when the story is retold. There may be some hope: after all, the murder of Susan Long in Norfolk in 1970 is being re-examined as detectives work on DNA found in garments, and the blood-group of the killer is a rare one. The original work of taking 3,700 statements may not have been in vain. Something of the same kind of procedure may not be impossible in the case of Walter Taylor. The local community would dearly love this case to be resolved. A A Clarke, writing on the case in his book, *Killers at Large* (1994) gives an analysis of the people seen at the sites near to the scene of death, and there are so many individuals listed that one would be sanguine about locating a person around the town today who has strong memories of some of the movements of people around Ashby on that fateful night for poor Walter.

CHAPTER 47

Destination: Lucy Tower and Greetwell Road

Only twenty-seven miles south of Scunthorpe, Lincoln was always going to be the place where many of the North Lincolnshire criminals ended their days. There were lock-ups and houses of correction across the north of the county, but for the desperate, amoral characters who took people's lives through anger or hatred, the last stopping-place from late Victorian times was the condemned cell in Lincoln prison on Greetwell Road.

Before the new prison, Lincoln Castle had served the purpose, and in the sixty-two years in which the Castle was the official place of execution, forty-four men and women were hanged there, in the tower at Cobb Hall, where today visitors park their cars before starting a tourist walk of the historical sites. People in Lincolnshire had been executed in the early years of the nineteenth century for such things as stealing animals or forgery of the coins of the realm. The last hanging in Lincoln for an offence other than wilful murder was, in fact, a rape committed not far from Scunthorpe, at Blyborough (a few miles south of Kirton Lindsey). This was when a young woman called Frances Elston, who was a domestic servant at Pilham, was walking home when she was attacked and raped by teenager, Thomas Knapton.

Relating the story of that institution also means placing the hangmen in the tale: from the brisk Calcraft to the mysteriously unknown executioner who dismissed of the last man hanged in Lincoln, Wasyl Gnypiuk, in 1961, their story completes the picture of several of the killers whose deeds have been recounted here.

Before the new prison was built in 1872 and the professional hangman Marwood came into his new role, murderers in the county could expect to be in the incapable hands of some notoriously inept characters entrusted with the humane exit from this world. For instance, in a village only fifteen miles south of Scunthorpe, in 1850, a seventeen-year-old girl, Eliza Smalley, poisoned her mistress with arsenic, placing it in her coffee. She boiled a gill-full in the large coffee-pot kept simmering in the kitchen. Eliza would have been a customer of the official hangman, William Calcraft (who worked from 1829 to 1874).

Hanging was certainly not a fine art: Calcraft often had to scuttle down to the lower level and tug the legs of his clients to hasten death. Some may have thought him a man who botched the job, but evidence is not reliable. One witness noted that he was 'a kind, benevolent and reserved old man' who wore a skull cap when doing his trade. He was well paid, and if he had to journey up to Lincoln from London to do a job, he was paid the large sum of £10. But the Lincolnshire man, William Marwood, from 1874 until James Berry took over, was a different type. He saw the post of executioner as being highly skilled and professional, and even made his own business-cards. He conceived of the 'long drop' which was a more humane way of handling a hanging. He was born in Horncastle in 1818 and did his first hanging at Lincoln Castle. He was sarcastic about Calcraft, saying, 'He hanged them – I execute them!' Marwood insisted that he had improved everything done in that line of work: 'I believe I spare suffering

---

WM. MARWOOD

EXECUTIONER

C H U R C H   L A N E

HORNCASTLE

LINCOLNSHIRE, ENGLAND

Marwood's professional calling-card.

better than anyone else. The old plan was to kill by strangling: mine is dislocation.'

The first criminal to experience the new 'long drop' was William Berry in 1872. He was the son of a Boston man, and had made a new life for himself in Staffordshire, but he came back to Boston, and there he developed a crazy obsessional jealousy about his wife and this inevitably led to his murdering her.

When the Bradford man, James Berry, took over the post in 1884, he paid a visit to Lincoln and disposed of Arthur Spencer in 1891. Spencer was only twenty-two and had fallen in love with a widow older than himself; she rebuffed him and he turned violent. He shot her at point blank, but they bungled his attempt at suicide. Amazingly, the muzzle placed in his mouth and discharged, sent the bullet out of the back of his neck and he survived.

Berry's other visit to Lincoln was to execute a Grimsby sailor, Richard Insole, in 1887. He had killed his wife in a fit of jealousy. By the end of the nineteenth century, the death cell at Greetwell Road had been visited by three hangmen, and some of the men figuring in the Scunthorpe stories were seen out of this world in the death cell there. The last man from the Scunthorpe area to hang in Lincoln was Kenneth Roberts, whose story has been told already. But Lincoln prison has another interesting story with regard to the last hangman employed there: this was Syd Dearnley, who came to the prison for the job interview in 1948. The Governor, Brigadier Paton-Walsh, wrote that he should come 'to be medically examined and interviewed with a view to ascertaining your fitness for the post of assistant executioner.' He did so, and at the interview, when he spoke about hobbies, he confessed to enjoy pheasant shooting in Clumber Park.

But it is hard to think lightly about anything to do with hanging a man. At Lincoln prison, the arrangements and ritual were no different to most other prisons with a calendar of executions on their records. Marwood and his successors, the Pierrepoint family and later Steve Wade, became familiar with the sequence of events before the lever was pulled and the condemned person fell to the lower level, their asphyxiation very rapid.

Finally, where there has been so much death and misery, one might expect stories of paranormal happenings. It may come as no surprise to learn that in Lincoln prison, there have been numerous sightings of a figure in the administration block: he is reputed to be the restless spirit of Frederick Nodder, a killer hanged there in 1937 for the murder of little Mona Tinsley in Newark. The offices are built over what used to be the prison graveyard.

In the story of the killer Travis in Kirton, the legend now around the area is that around a five-barred gate on Leonard Field, no grass would grow on the spot where Kirton farmer John Copeman was savagely killed in 1847. One tradition says that at the spot where this happened, a roadman kept the area grass-free, as people would come to stare and take a less than healthy interest in the murder site. Copeman's body was first found lying in the Grayingham road, close to the Kirton side of the gate in Leonard's Field.

How men from around Axholme, Scunthorpe and Barton must have dreaded the short trip south down the Roman road, to the city where so many had breathed their last at the hands of the law.

Sources

Books

S Andrews (ed.), *Bygone Lincolnshire* 2 vols, A Brown, 1891

Elizabeth Armstrong (ed.), *An Industrial Island: A History of Scunthorpe*, Scunthorpe Borough Museum and Art Gallery, 1981

A A Clarke, *The Groaning Gallows*, Arton Books, 1994

R and K Cooke, *Scunthorpe*, Stroud, 1997

Rupert Creed and Averil Coult, *Steeltown*, Hutton Press, 1990

B J Davey, *Rural Crime in the Eighteenth Century: North Lincolnshire 1740–1780*, University of Hull Press, 1994

John J Eddleston, *The Encyclopaedia of Executions*, John Blake, 2002

Colin Ella, *Myths and Legends of the Isle of Axholme*, Chronicle Pubs, 2003

Bert Fryer, *Recollections of a Country Copper 1936–1966*, The author, 1996

Adrian Gray, *Crime and criminals in Victorian Lincolnshire*, Paul Watkins, 1993

Nick Lyons, *Scunthorpe: A Photographic History of Your Town*, Black Horse Books, 2002

Hamish Maxwell-Stewart and Susan Hood, *Pack of Thieves? 52 Port Arthur Lives*, Port Arthur Authority, 2001

Geoffrey Moorhouse, *The Pilgrimage of Grace*, Phoenix, 2003

David Newton and Martin Smith, *Stamford Mercury: Three Centuries of Newspaper Publishing*, Shaun Tyas, 1999

N Pevsner, *The Buildings of England: Lincolnshire*, Penguin 1964 edition

Sian Rees, *The Floating Brothel*, Review, 2001

Tony Satchell, *For Better or Worse. Convict Lives shaped by Transportation*, Craftsman Press, 2003

Judith Spelman, *Lincolnshire Bedside Book*, Dovecote Press, 2003

Geoff Tibballs, *The Murder Guide to Great Britain*, Box Tree, 1994

Periodicals and Newspapers
Lincolnshire Echo, special supplements
Lincolnshire Gazette
Lincolnshire Life
Lincolnshire Poacher
Scunthorpe Evening Telegraph
The Epworth Bells

Booklets and Monographs
Convicts of Lincolnshire, compiled by C L Anderson,
    Lincolnshire County Council, 1988
Mike Cliff, *A History of Brigg Fairs*, The author, 2001
A J Kerswill, *A History of North Kelsey*, The author, 1992

Index